MUNSTER
HURLING LEGENDS

' ... a zestfully written, hugely entertaining account ...
of that near-mystical phenomenon known
as Munster hurling'
Irish Independent

' ... a real treasure for lovers of the ancient game'
Gaelic World

'... a superb book, full of colour, incidents and stories to tell'
Clare County Express

'... full of delightful insights'
Irish News

EAMONN SWEENEY was born in the nearly hurling-free county of Sligo – a deficiency remedied by his hurling-mad father from Kilkenny. He has written on GAA for the *Irish Examiner* for a number of years and is the author of two novels, *The Photograph* and *Waiting for the Healer*, a book on soccer, *There's Only One Red Army*, and a play, *Bruen's Twist*. He also regularly broadcasts on RTÉ radio and television on a wide variety of topics. Hurling has been his passion for many years, and ever since moving to the southernmost county the Hurling Championship has been the premier sporting event of the year for him.

OTHER SPORTS BOOKS FROM
THE O'BRIEN PRESS

Joey Dunlop, King of the Roads
Munster, Rugby Giants
The Gaffers, Mick McCarthy, Roy Keane and the team they built
For details of all O'Brien Press books, see www.obrien.ie

MUNSTER
HURLING LEGENDS
Seven Decades of the Greatest Teams, Players and Games

EAMONN SWEENEY

THE O'BRIEN PRESS
DUBLIN

First published in hardback in 2002 by The O'Brien Press Ltd,
20 Victoria Road, Dublin 6, Ireland.
Tel: +353 1 4923333; Fax: +353 1 4922777
E-mail: books@obrien.ie
Website: www.obrien.ie
First published in paperback, as an updated edition, in 2003.

ISBN: 0-86278-846-3

British Library Cataloguing-in-Publication Data
Sweeney, Eamonn, 1968-
Munster hurling legends: seven decades of the greatest teams, players and games.-2nd ed.
1. Hurling (Game) - Ireland - Munster - History - 20th century
2. Hurling players - Ireland - Munster - Biography
I. Title
796.3'5

2 3 4 5 6 7 8
03 04 05 06 07 08 09

Editing, typesetting, layout: The O'Brien Press Ltd
Design: Frank Murphy, Designit
Printing: GraphyCEMS

A C K N O W L E D G E M E N T S

First, and foremost, to my partner Siobhán Cadogan and our daughter, Emily, for exercising the infinite patience required to live with a writer. Thanks also to the other members of my family for their usual encouragement. And to Ronnie Bellew for good advice and companionship, and to Dermot Crowe and Denis Walsh for valuable help. I consulted a number of books while writing this one. I'd particularly like to recommend Val Dorgan's *Christy Ring, A Personal Portrait, Beyond the Tunnel* by Nicky English with Vincent Hogan, *Raising the Banner* by John Scally, *Hooked* by Justin McCarthy with Kieran Shannon, Norman Freeman's *Great Hurling Matches 1956–75 and 1976–91* and Seamus J King's marvellous *A History of Hurling*.

There are two people without whom this book would not have seen the light of day. Rachel Pierce as editor has been a model of help, advice and forbearance. I thank her with all my heart. And at the *Irish Examiner*, Ann Kearney's help with the provision of photographs was remarkable and cheerfully went beyond the bounds of what I had the right to expect. She is, in a sense, the co-author of this book. I would also like to thank Frank Murphy for his marvellous design. The book could not have been published without the cooperation of the *Irish Examiner*, and I thank the staff of the library there for their exemplary assistance. To my mind, the glory of this book is the wealth of photographs it contains, and I'd like to pay tribute to the *Irish Examiner* photographers whose work is contained here, particularly Des Barry, Dan Linehan and Denis Minihane, an extremely talented trio I've been lucky enough to work with on occasion. Thanks also to Tony Leen, without whom I wouldn't have had any association with The Paper, and to Colm O'Connor and Declan Colley as well.

Finally, thanks to the hurlers of Ireland for investing even the rainiest summers with magic.

C O N T E N T S

INTRODUCTION

For decades now a Tipperary town with only a few thousand inhabitants has routinely crammed 50,000 people into its narrow streets on one special summer Sunday. Munster final day in Thurles is a perfect analogy for the GAA's effect on Irish life. Like the Munster final, the GAA is almost too big for its surroundings, drawing disproportionately large crowds for a small country. It is the kind of association that can draw 20,000 people to a club match played between two teams representing parishes whose total population is one-fifth of that number. Attendances at the big inter-county games are equal to those at the biggest of Serie A and Premiership soccer matches, despite the huge difference in population size. Thurles shouldn't be able to cope with all the people who throng the streets on Munster final day. But it does. And the GAA shouldn't have become the biggest sporting organisation in the country. But it has.

Looking at its origins, the Association's success was far from inevitable, because if ever there was an inauspicious birth it was that of the GAA on 1 November 1884. Only seven people are recorded in the minutes as being present at the meeting in the billiards room of Miss Hayes Commercial Hotel, Thurles (although a further six men are sometimes said to have attended as well). The seven who did turn up were: Michael Cusack, Maurice Davin, John Wyse-Power, John McKay, JK Bracken, Joseph O'Ryan and Thomas St George McCarthy, and in all likelihood they probably did not know what they were starting. The GAA entered the world not with a bang but with a barely audible whimper. The founders didn't even bother to set a date for the second meeting.

Cusack, who provided the model for The Citizen in Joyce's *Ulysses*, was the man responsible for initiating the meeting. A teacher from Clare who lived in Dublin and was a member of the Irish Republican Brotherhood (IRB), he had written an article in the *United Irishman* newspaper calling for an Irish national sporting body to be established. Davin, from Carrick-on-Suir, was one of the leading athletes of the day. Wyse-Power was the editor of the *Leinster Leader* newspaper and also a member of the IRB. McCarthy, on the other hand, was a Tipperaryman who was a District Inspector in the Royal

Irish Constabulary (RIC). Bracken was a building contractor from Templemore, O'Ryan was a solicitor from Carrick-on-Suir and McKay was a Belfast journalist working for the *Cork Examiner* (now *Irish Examiner*).

As the sporting septet left Hayes Hotel on that dark, cold, wet night, they must have been assailed by doubts about their new venture. Soccer and rugby were increasingly popular in the country and, difficult though it is to believe at this remove, even cricket was making inroads. The GAA, in opposition, could offer the ancient and now extinct sport of hurling, alongside Gaelic football – a game largely of its own devising. Small wonder then that the main hope of Cusack (who would become the first President of the Association) and his *confrères* was to take control of the then hugely popular sport of athletics. Hurling and football were, for the moment, secondary concerns. Look at the name of the Association.

The Big Day Out: corporate hospitality 1930s style at the 1934 Munster semi-final between Cork and Limerick in Thurles.

The start might have been shaky, but nonetheless it was soon obvious that the GAA, and hurling, in particular, had captured the public imagination. Within a year clubs had been set up in Dublin, Offaly, Galway, Tipperary, Kilkenny, Antrim and Cork. By 1887 over 10,000 people were turning up at Elm Park, Dublin, to see Galway defeat Wexford. On 1 April 1888, Thurles, representing Tipperary, became the first All-Ireland champions by defeating Meelick of Galway. Soon football and hurling were the country's most popular games.

Cusack and his cohorts would have seen the rise of football and hurling to pre-eminence as proof that the games corresponded to a deep-seated need in the Irish soul. Perhaps a better, though not altogether different explanation can be found in the words of Louis Marcus, the film-maker who made a masterly documentary about Christy Ring, the supreme hurler of the twentieth century. 'Ring,' said Marcus, 'was a figure of beauty. Watching him, the crowds enjoyed a poetry they did not find anywhere else.' The Ireland of Ring's time was a place of economic hardship, religious repression and rural stagnation. That beleaguered land found its heroes on the pitch in places like Croke Park, the Cork Athletic Grounds and in Semple Stadium, Thurles. The GAA was Ireland's Hollywood – a place where dreams were created and stars were born. The great Munster finals were part sporting event and part ritual, more akin to the Palio horse race in Siena, or to the annual bull-running event in Pamplona than they were to FA Cup ties.

'FROM BISHOPS TO TRAMPS OFF THE ROAD'

When I came to write this book, I began by taking the Cork–Dublin train and stepping off at Thurles. It was a chilly January day and at ten o'clock in the morning there was little movement in the streets – it looked like any other small town. But the very silence helped me to imagine what it must have been like on Munster final day in the 1940s and 1950s, when the signs advertising meat teas went up in the front windows of houses in Friar Street and Parnell Street, and when, to quote the writer Daniel Corkery, 'there were all sorts of individuals present, from bishops to tramps off the road.' Above all, I tried to think of what Liberty Square must have looked like in 1944 when, despite transport restrictions caused by The Emergency, huge crowds turned out to watch two legendary matches between Limerick and Cork, making their way to Thurles by bike, by horse-and-cart and on foot, some of them even sleeping in the town square the night before.

I could easily imagine those days because, although the Ireland of today would be almost unrecognisable to the supporters of 1944, the scene in Thurles on Munster final day would not be. Hayes Hotel is still there and is still packed to the rafters on match days. The young spectators today don't wear suits and might not have managed to get

Mass that morning, but the fortunes of their team in the Munster final matters every bit as much to them as it did to their forebears. Because, remarkably, in an Ireland obsessed with modernity and terrified of being considered backward for embracing the traditional, the GAA has actually grown stronger. An infamous *Irish Independent* article in 1985, written by journalist Kevin O'Connor, painted a picture of the future, with the new, trendy Irish forsaking Croke Park for the heady delights of Lansdowne Road. As a piece of prophecy it ranks with the comment by the record company executive who disdained to sign The Beatles on the grounds that 'groups with guitars are on the way out.'

Whatever else changes in Ireland, the people's love for hurling continues unabated. Maybe that doesn't have much to do with soul, or art, or national identity. Maybe hurling endures in the affections simply because it is one of the most exciting games in the world, because there is nothing quite like it in its combination of the balletic and the bruising. Or perhaps it does hit some chord within us, its very uniqueness giving supporters a chance to indulge in the least harmful form of national pride there is: sporting pride. Either way, the Munster hurling final has long been the most stirring, the most intriguing, the most resonant, the most romantic, the most heroic sporting fixture in the country. It was made that way by great matches, by great players and, above all, by great teams. This book is a tribute to, a story about and an examination of those teams and the magic they worked.

Eamonn Sweeney
August 2002

The old Cork Athletic Grounds, forerunner to today's Páirc Uí Chaoímh, sees Limerick take on Waterford in the 1934 Munster final.

fifty-eight, drawing four and losing just three. A less strenuous schedule might have given them that extra bit of freshness required for All-Ireland wins in 1935 and 1937.

Sixty-five games in four-and-a-half years would be a gruelling schedule for a modern-day player, but it bordered on the suicidal for players in an era when the desk job and the day off work were almost alien concepts. Like Ahane, the Limerick team were noted for their eagerness to support good causes through tournament games. This was especially tough on those hurlers who made their living from farming. Mickey Cross, Limerick's outstanding wing-back, quit the game for good after the 1937 Munster final against Tipperary. He had played that day in a state of considerable sorrow after a fire that morning had destroyed his stables and killed some of his best horses. And Peter Cregan retired early because of his work as a farm manager. For every big match he had to pay a woman two shillings to milk his cows – a sacrifice that eventually became too much.

The greatest Limerick team of all time set out on their long road in 1933 when they upset Munster champions Clare in the first round. That match was most notable for the incredible extravagance of chartering a train to bring just two hurlers – Christy O'Brien of Limerick and Clare's Jim Houlihan – to the match after they had played a club game in Dublin earlier in the day. A crowd of 30,000 saw Limerick beat an over-the-hill Cork by 2-9 to 1-6 in the Munster semi, thereby setting up a Munster final against the unlikely opposition of Waterford.

Although hooliganism has never been a serious problem in hurling, the crowds of the 1930s and 1940s were far less well-behaved than today's supporters and had a more hands-on approach to the game. Pitch invasions, sometimes sparked by overcrowding, sometimes by a refereeing decision and sometimes by the wish to influence the result, were not uncommon. And so it turned out that the 1933 Munster final, although played in the Cork Athletic Grounds, was decided in Clonmel.

The decisive incident occurred with just eight minutes left, when Limerick were leading by 3-7 to 1-2. A punch-up between the players led to the crowd invading the pitch and the match having to be abandoned. A meeting of the Munster Council in Ryan's Hotel, Clonmel, decided that Limerick should be awarded the title. Their All-Ireland final opposition would be Kilkenny, experienced and with several survivors from the team that had taken Cork to two replays before losing in the classic 1931 All-Ireland final. One of those survivors was Lory Meagher, the Tullaroan farmer still regarded as the finest midfielder ever to play the game. They had come from twelve points down against Dublin at half-time in the Leinster final to win by six points, and had defeated Limerick in that year's National League final. Kilkenny were hot favourites, but Limerick were expected to mount a huge challenge. The crowd of 45,000 at Croke Park was the biggest ever for an Irish sporting event. Another 5,000 people were locked outside. Limerick's pull on the affections of the public was already obvious.

Kilkenny's greater experience proved vital and with time running out they were 0-7 to 0-5 ahead. Limerick went all out for a winning goal, but were driven back time and again before Kilkenny put the match beyond doubt – Johnny Dunne juggling through the defence before bulleting a shot past Paddy Scanlan to give the Cats a 1-7 to 0-6 victory. Limerick, though, had now developed a taste for Croke Park on All-Ireland day. They won the 1934 Munster Championship with some comfort, though Scanlan had to pull off some wonderful saves to see them past Cork 3-4 to 2-2 in the semi-final before they beat Waterford 4-8 to 2-5 in the provincial final. At the unusual venue of Roscrea, Galway were disposed of in the All-Ireland semi-final by six points, and only Dublin stood in Limerick's way now. It would be a strange final for Limerick left half-back

No quarter given or requested in the 1934 Munster final between Limerick and Waterford.

Garret Howard. He had won three All-Ireland medals with Dublin before the GAA's rules were changed to allow players working in other parts of the country to play for their county of origin.

So the 1934 final looked set to be a dramatic event. As it transpired, there was a remarkable similarity between the first, drawn game and the replay as both games finished with a flourish. In the first match Dublin trailed by five points with five minutes left, but they came back to draw 2-7 to 3-4.

Limerick's preparations for the replay were disturbed when the talismanic Paddy Scanlan was forced to withdraw through illness. So Tom Shinny of Fedamore came in to play the most important match of his career. In the replay, with two minutes to go, the sides were tied at Limerick 4-0, Dublin 2-6. Then Mick Mackey and Jackie O'Connell struck points and Dave Clohessy his fourth goal of the game to give the Munster champions victory. The crowd went wild. Thirty thousand people lined the streets as a triumphant Limerick brought the Liam McCarthy Cup through the city to the Imperial Hotel in Catherine Street.

If anything, Limerick looked even stronger the following year for the 1935 campaign. Mackey's display when they trounced Cork 3-12 to 2-3 in the Munster semi-final in Thurles is regarded as one of the greatest in the history of the game. He scored a goal inside two minutes as Limerick went six points up in as many minutes. Then Limerick suffered a grave blow when defender Paddy Clohessy was sent off. In the reshuffle, Mackey moved to midfield and completely dominated the rest of the game. The match was also notable for a remarkable interlude when Cork player Tommy Kelly was injured so badly in a collision with Limerick midfielder Mick Ryan that players, officials and the entire crowd knelt as he received the Last Rites on the pitch. The silence was all the more eerie given the raucous excitement that had preceded it. The power of prayer evidently worked a miracle because Kelly recovered to the extent that he was discharged from hospital the next day.

An apparently unstoppable Limerick next defeated Tipperary by 5-5 to 1-4 in the Munster final and looked ready to avenge their defeat of 1933 against Kilkenny in the All-Ireland final. The hold of this charismatic team on the general public was well illustrated when the final attracted a record crowd of 46,591. But once more Kilkenny got the better of the Munster champions, coming through by 2-5 to 2-4 in a downpour.

Before the match, Kilkenny had been written off as too old, but they led by 1-3 to 1-2 at the break and had moved five points clear by the end of the third-quarter. Limerick launched attack after attack in the final fifteen minutes, but Mick Mackey's final effort to save the game was foiled by Paddy Larkin, whose son, Fan, and grandson, Philly, would also win All-Ireland medals with Kilkenny. But it showed the affection in which the team were held at home that the players were still carried shoulder-high to the Imperial Hotel when they got back to the city.

LIMERICK AT THEIR PEAK

The following year, 1936, arguably saw Limerick at their peak. They began the season by embarking on an American tour and were awarded a bye to the provincial final because of this. They departed from Cobh on May 9 on the *Manhattan* and returned a month later on the *Washington*. Around 40,000 fans saw them defeat a New York team made up of Irish expatriates.

During the tour, Mick Mackey sustained an injury to his right knee. The Tipperary defence were a physical bunch and would pounce on any sign of weakness in the opposition's star player. Mackey's love of carrying the ball right into the heart of the defence made him enough of a target as it was. And he wasn't the kind of man who would change his style of play just because he was injured. Limerick hit on the novel idea of putting a large bandage on Mackey's uninjured left knee. The ruse must have paid off because Mackey, in his first game as captain, played the game of his life and scored an incredible 5-3 as Limerick won by 8-5 to 4-6. Galway were next for the chop and departed in irregular fashion, walking off the pitch in Roscrea with fifteen minutes left to play because they claimed Limerick were too rough. The fact that they were eleven points down at the time might have had something to do with their unscheduled departure as well.

Mick Mackey has a word with the Galway players in a 1939 National League match.

Hurling surrealism: first prize of a time-machine trip back to the 1940s for anyone who can tell us what's happening here in the 1940 Munster final between Cork and Limerick in Thurles.

Kilkenny again stood in Limerick's way in the All-Ireland final, but this time there was no mistake and Limerick powered past them 5-6 to 1-5 to prove conclusively that they were the best team in the country. Star of the show was young Jackie Power, making his début for his county and scoring two goals with the *sangfroid* of an old veteran. Paddy Clohessy's display at wing-back was also exceptional.

The signs that Limerick's reign might be drawing to a close were apparent in the 1937 Munster semi-final at Clonmel when unfancied Waterford, inspired by John Keane, the county's greatest-ever player, would have been out of sight but for three great saves by Scanlan. The underdogs still led by two points going into the last minute before a Dave Clohessy goal edged Limerick home. Waterford complained bitterly that too much injury time had been played. Limerick had been given a fright, but the champions were still hot favourites to make it five Munsters in a row when they met Tipperary in the final. Instead, Tipperary came through by 6-6 to 4-6, although Mick Mackey was again outstanding. This was the final played in the aftermath of the fire at Mickey Cross's, which arguably affected his team-mates as well as the player himself.

This defeat took the old sheen of provincial invulnerability off Limerick, and they were easily beaten by Cork in the first round in 1938. The following year the same counties drew 40,986 people to Thurles – an increase of more than 10,000 on previous

Mick Mackey receives the McCarthy Cup after Limerick defeated Kilkenny 3-7 to 1-7 in the 1940 All-Ireland final.

record for a Munster final. They delivered a classic game for their devoted fans, but this time Limerick were the team caught at the line, despite a monumental display by Scanlan. A last-gasp goal by Cork gave the Rebels a 4-3 to 3-4 win. A dispute in the county championship had meant that Paddy Clohessy was not playing that day, something that may have cost Limerick the game.

ESCAPE IN KILLARNEY

And that, to most observers, was largely that for Limerick – a great team that had gone over the hill. That presumption only made their final triumph in 1940 all the more remarkable. They didn't look like potential champions when they were held to a draw by Waterford in the Munster semi-final in Killarney. They only escaped that day because of two individual goals by Jackie Power and a storming display by Mick Mackey when he was switched to centre half-back. And it took another late rally to give them a 3-5 to 3-3 win in the replay.

Limerick, however, upped their performance to draw the Munster final at 4-3 to Cork's 3-6 – their old nemesis needing a last-minute point from John Quirke to level. But at half-time in the replay they looked a busted flush, held scoreless for the entire half by an outstanding Cork defence. Their only consolation was that Cork had not built up the large lead their possession merited.

Limerick were a changed team in the second-half. Timmy Ryan took over at midfield and Mick Mackey got the revival underway with a point from a seventy. In the space of a few minutes, Jackie Power, Paddy McMahon and Dick Stokes scored goals to put Limerick comfortably ahead. A stunned Cork replied with goals from Jack Lynch and Quirke, but with Mick Mackey dropping back to help out his defence, Ryan continuing to rule the middle of the pitch and John Mackey and Mick Kennedy (ironically enough a Tipperaryman) excelling themselves, Limerick held on grimly.

The Limerick team that defeated Kilkenny in the 1940 All-Ireland in Croke Park.

Paddy Scanlan, Limerick's legendary goalkeeper.

Interventionist spectators were to make their task even more difficult once again. A challenge on Cork's Micka Brennan by Paddy Scanlan, which resulted in Brennan having to be carried off, led to a pitch invasion. However, the cunning Cork followers left the Limerick goalmouth clear to give their team a chance to score the winning goal in the midst of the confusion, but Limerick managed to put the *sliothar* out in time. It took ten minutes for the gardaí to clear the pitch. In the last minute Lynch had a chance to win the game, but Scanlan was equal to his shot and Limerick held on 3-3 to 2-4. It was perhaps their finest win of all because it was the least expected. Galway went under next in the All-Ireland semi-final, and Kilkenny were the opposition once more in the final.

On 1 September 1940, nearly 50,000 spectators were there to watch this last great reckoning between the two outstanding teams of the era. Early in the second-half Kilkenny led by 1-6 to 1-2 and Mick Mackey was sent on his travels again, dispatched to midfield where he proceeded to dominate the game. He inspired Limerick to a 3-7 to 1-7 victory, which wrote a fitting coda to their success story. It more than made up for the extra titles which might have been theirs when the team was at its peak. The jubilant fans who watched their heroes being ferried to Cruise's Hotel in Limerick City on trucks provided by the Irish Army could hardly have imagined that it would be thirty-three years before the county would again hold aloft the McCarthy Cup. Yet even then there would be a connection to this great team – Jackie Power coached the 1973 side that took up the baton from the boys of 1940.

The 1940 team were:

Paddy Scanlan

Jim McCarthy   **Mick Hickey**   **Mick Kennedy**

Tommy Cooke   **Paddy Clohessy**   **Peter Cregan**

Timmy Ryan   **Jim Roche**

John Mackey   **Mick Mackey**   **Dick Stokes**

Ned Clarke   **Paddy McMahon**   **Jackie Power**

They say that the second-best is never remembered, but Mick Mackey proved that adage wrong. He is almost unanimously reckoned to be the second-best hurler of all time. The only man who could be said to have bested him was the unparalleled Christy Ring. But Mackey is remembered with the same adulation, respect and awe by those who witnessed this master of the game in action.

What is most interesting about Mackey is that in some respects he was the opposite of Ring. While Ring inspired awe and respect, Mackey inspired affection. Ring's single-minded pursuit of excellence and obvious determination to win at all costs weren't seen as entirely fitting in a country where self-deprecation and modesty were deemed cardinal virtues. You could say that Ring regarded hurling as an art, that he was the sport's Samurai warrior with a hurley instead of a sword. Mackey, on the other hand, treated it as a sport. He was a cavalier, and he certainly earned his nickname: The Playboy of the Southern World. As his team-mate Jackie O'Connell put it, Mackey enjoyed himself on the pitch and played with abandon. Hurling was just one part of his life – a passion, yes, but not the sum of the man – while Ring's life was devoted entirely to the game. In Mackey's own words: 'I was a cool class of a customer. It was good *craic*. Maybe Ring didn't get the same fun out of it.'

It was the ESB van-driver from Castleconnell whom the crowds loved, a player whose place in the affections of the public hasn't been equalled since. He played with a smile on his face and seemed to embark on his famous solo runs just for the joy it gave to the spectators. He was extraordinarily powerful, standing over six-feet tall and weighing a well-muscled thirteen stone, and many opponents were in awe of his physical appearance. Ring told a story of how a Cork player punched Mackey and 'Mackey went twice round the pitch after him and the only thing that stopped [the Cork player] running home to Cork was the paling around the ground.' All the same, Mackey had a reputation for sportsmanship. In one match against Waterford, he and his marker, Christy Moylan, twice had to be separated after flare-ups. But when Mackey was handed an orange by a Limerick mentor, he threw one half of it to Moylan.

He is regarded as the most natural and most instinctive hurler of all time, which perhaps has something to do with the fact that he was taught the game by his father, John 'Tyler' Mackey, one of the greatest players of the preceding generation. Thanks to his ministrations, Mackey Junior could leave defenders for dead with a turn, was able to absorb all kinds of punishment on his way through, and when moving at pace was next to unstoppable. Pulling with equal facility on his left and right sides, picking the *sliothar* under extreme pressure and all the other fundamental skills seemed to come naturally to him.

Mackey was an individualist in many ways, refusing to abide by the rules of the GAA that forbade players to attend foreign games. Terrified of the reaction that would greet a suspension for Mackey, the Limerick County Board made him a member of their Vigilance Committee. The committee had members in every county and it was their task to attend 'foreign' games – rugby and soccer – ostensibly to see if any GAA members were present and report their names back to the Association. By all accounts, Mick Mackey was extremely vigilant and attended every game he possibly could.

Mick Mackey's presence on the pitch drew several thousand extra spectators to the games. He was one of the country's great popular entertainers – a sporting equivalent of the silver-screen heroes played by the likes of Errol Flynn and Tyrone Power. He died in 1982, aged seventy, after a long illness. Limerick has not seen his like since. Indeed, where has?

C H A P T E R   T W O

THE GREATEST?

Cork, 1940–1946

Munster Champions 1942, 1943, 1944, 1946

All-Ireland Champions 1941, 1942, 1943, 1944, 1946

The All-Ireland final of 1939 was played on 3 September, the same day England and France declared war on Germany, and the Second World War began. Though remaining neutral, Ireland was indirectly affected by the conflict. The tribulations of the population were miniscule compared with the sufferings endured throughout the rest of Europe, but The Emergency was nonetheless a time of austerity, fuel shortages, rationing and transport bans. The GAA was affected too as attendances nose-dived due to petrol shortages. By 1944, however, the crowds were as big as ever because supporters reverted to the kinds of methods which had got their forefathers to the big games: their bicycles, or their own two feet. It was a time when the GAA follower took a trip into the past in order to make the trip to the games. And it was, indisputably, Cork's decade.

Was the Cork team of the 1940s the greatest Ireland has ever seen? By one important measure they undoubtedly were: they remain the only team ever to win four All-Ireland hurling titles in a row. That statistic might be expected to speak for itself, but some doubt has been cast over the worth of those championship wins. Mick Mackey, for example, stuck stoutly to his claim that his Limerick team of the previous decade were the greatest side of all time. He derided the Cork four-in-a-row as having come at the expense of a Dublin team that had descended the far side of the hill, and an Antrim team that had got into the final only by a fluke. There is also a huge questionmark over the bizarre 1941 championship when Cork lost the Munster final after winning the All-Ireland. But despite the begrudgers, and no matter what the opposition, to win four All-Ireland titles in a row is a salutary achievement, and one that proved beyond the other great teams gathered in this book, some of them boasting the finest players who ever wielded a hurley.

And there is another, though less often considered statistic that suggests the Cork team of the time dominated domestic hurling to an extent unprecedented before and unmatched since. The story of this Cork team is bookended by defeats in two of the classic All-Ireland finals, those of 1939 and 1947. Defeat on both occasions was by a single point. So it is not an impossible stretch to imagine that, with a couple of lucky breaks, Cork could have won an incredible seven All-Irelands out of nine.

The calm before the storm: Cork and Kilkenny march in the pre-match parade prior to the All-Ireland hurling final on the day the Second World War began, 3 September 1939. Cork lost by a point, 2-7 to 3-3, but went on to win five of the next seven finals.

The team of this unforgettable decade had an ever-present backbone of nine players who played in all four finals: Christy Ring, Jack Lynch, Din Joe Buckley, Jim Young,

Willie Murphy, Paddy O'Donovan, Batt Thornhill, Alan Lotty and John Quirke. Five of them were from Glen Rovers, the city side that had won ten Cork championships in a row between 1932 and 1941. Unashamedly working class and fanatically proud of what they felt was a unique 'Spirit of the Glen', they were one of the most remarkable club sides in the history of the game. When they won a county title they would celebrate wildly in the centre of the city before retreating back to their home turf of Blackpool, their route marked by blazing tar barrels. Although the Cork team was mainly city-based, there were rural members: Thornhill was from the North Cork town of Buttevant, Willie Murphy came from Ballincollig in the Lee Valley, Lotty from Glanmire to the east of the city and Con Murphy, who joined the team in 1941, played for

Willie 'Long Puck' Murphy of Ballincollig and Cork, one of the great corner-backs and one of nine Cork players with the unique distinction of winning four All-Ireland senior hurling medals in a row.

Valley Rovers, a club based to the west in Inishannon, a place later lovingly described by its most famous resident, Alice Taylor.

The man behind this formidable team, their dynamic manager, was a crucially important factor in their success but remains a largely unsung hero. In the era of all-powerful County Boards and management by committee, he was an anomalous figure. But then nothing about Jim 'Tough' Barry made him a typical inter-county hurling supremo. Very few hurling managers have, after all, sung with the Carl Rosa Opera Company. Nor have many managers trained the county team for over forty years as Barry did – he was involved in the All-Ireland wins of both 1926 and 1966. It was quite a record for a man who had never played hurling at a serious level, for the playing career of the remarkable manager behind the four-in-a-row team had stretched just as far as junior hurling with the famous Blackrock club, though he had also been a successful boxer and diver.

In the 1940s managers weren't the powerful figures they are now. The real power lay with the County Board officials. The advent of the modern tactical mastermind, the undisputed leader of the team, occurred only in the 1970s when the GAA absorbed it from professional soccer. But Barry was nevertheless regarded by his players as having played an invaluable part in the four-in-a-row. He was the man who persuaded employers to release their players for training, who badgered the County Board to make sure the team got a good meal after matches, who ensured the grass on the training ground was cut to enable his skilful ball-players to express themselves fully. Barry kept interfering selectors away from his players and was even known to dip into his own pocket from time to time to help them out financially. His fierce loyalty to his players was also demonstrated when a coterie of Galway players vented their spleen by attacking Christy Ring in Barry's Hotel on the morning after the 1953 All-Ireland final, which Cork won. Barry had to be dissuaded from smashing down a door with a chair to get at Ring's tormenters.

'You can't miss me, I'll be wearing a hat.' Spectators at the National League final between Cork and Tipp in Cork, April 1940.

prodigy who might have been the best of them all. Certainly at the time he was regarded as an even better prospect than the legendary Christy Ring.

Kennefick was just seventeen years old when he made his début for the Cork senior team. Standing six-feet and two-inches tall and powerfully built, he was handed the apparently impossible task of marking Mick Mackey in the Munster semi-final. But he managed it. Just one year later he was lifting the Liam McCarthy Cup. There seemed to be nothing he couldn't accomplish, and he was young enough to do it all. But in the first round of the 1944 championship his wrist was broken by Tipperary player James Ryan. Kennefick never played for Cork again, but he did have the pleasure of seeing his son-in-law, Jimmy Barry-Murphy, become one of the biggest stars in the game in the 1970s and 1980s.

The other star player that year was Joe Kelly of Glen Rovers, the 'Barr's city rivals. He was only a couple of years out of minor but was already one of the fastest hurlers of all time. The Irish sprint champion, Kelly terrorised defences and thrilled crowds with his blistering pace. Like Kennefick, he quit the game before he reached his peak, choosing to

Sprint champion and brilliant corner-forward Joe Kelly of Cork takes on the Dublin defence in the 1944 All-Ireland final. Kelly was the star of the show as Cork completed the four-in-a-row with a 2-13 to 1-2 victory. Dublin keeper Jim Donegan keeps a watchful eye.

emigrate to New Zealand.

Now with three All-Ireland titles under their belt, Cork were probably still conscious that they hadn't been pushed to their utmost and that they had not figured in any game to match, for example, the 1940 Munster final. But 1944, their history-making year, would remedy those shortcomings. The games they will always be remembered for were known as The Great Bicycle Finals.

BY HOOK OR BY CROOK

Cork beat Tipperary in the Munster semi-final to set up a final clash with the perennial big draw, Limerick, who were enjoying another revival. Mick Mackey was a veteran by now but seemed to be playing better than ever. Wartime travel restrictions were biting hard, but the whole country talked about seeing Mackey and his team putting an end to Cork's four-in-a-row hopes in Thurles. On the Saturday afternoon before the game, all rail and bus services to Thurles were full. Hordes of cyclists began to head for the town in a huge convoy. Soon every bed in the town was filled and the overflow settled down for the night in Liberty Square, or in handy outhouses and haybarns. By the next morning the roads were black with bikes, carts and walkers, many of whom had taken Shanks's mare the whole forty miles from Limerick. The fact that it was one of the hottest days of the decade added to the carnival atmosphere.

Cork quickly went two goals up, but an inspired Mackey kept his side in the game all the way through, scoring points from impossible angles and setting up a series of attacks. It was the day when Cork centre half-back Con Murphy (who was later to become president of the GAA) saw Mackey power past him for two goals. After scoring the second, Mackey smiled at Murphy and told the twenty-two-year-old rookie that he'd surely be taken off now. Cork were put to the pin of their collar, but just when it looked as though Mackey had done enough to put Limerick through, Johnny Quirke, who had had the game of his life and ended up with a hat-trick, fired in a late goal to put Cork ahead. Limerick launched one last effort, which secured an equalising point from Dick Stokes to end the match, Cork 6-7, Limerick 4-13. So Cork, and Murphy, had survived to fight another day despite everything Limerick had thrown at them.

If anticipation had been high the first day, it was positively feverish for the replay. One sixty-five-year-old Corkman, Peter Ryan of Lisnagry, walked thirty-five miles to the game just to see the two go head to head. Limerick looked as though they'd learned most from the drawn match. They were five points clear entering the last quarter and with seven minutes left still held a 3-6 to 2-5 advantage. Then Mackey scored a goal, the Limerick fans went wild and the game seemed as good as over. But play was called back because Mackey had been fouled as he was going through. A free was awarded instead and Limerick missed it. The lack of an advantage rule would cost them dearly because this stroke of luck seemed to inspire Cork to one last Herculean effort. Jim Morrison's goal left just one point between the teams and Quirke obliged with an equalising point. The tension was unbearable at this stage and the crowd sensed that one moment of individual brilliance would be enough to win it. With one minute left, Mackey tried for the winning point. His shot hit the outside of the post and dropped wide.

THE MANTLE PASSES

Only seconds remained when Ring got the *sliothar* in his own half-back line, soloed past a succession of challenges and, from forty yards out, hammered a shot to the net.

History is made: Cork's captain, Sean Condon, with the McCarthy Cup after Cork make it four All-Irelands in a row in 1944.

Cork won by 4-6 to 3-6, and that final, dramatic minute of play marked the passing of the mantle of hurling's star player from Mackey to Ring.

How much those epics had taken out of Cork is shown by the fact that, minus the injured Lynch and Quirke, they nearly slipped up in the All-Ireland semi-final, just squeezing past Galway by 1-10 to 3-3 in Ennis. Only an eight-point contribution from Sean Condon prevented a huge upset. But Cork still weren't safely through – Galway had one last shot up their sleeves. The team's management went to Central Council and argued that one of their players had thrown a hurley at Condon as he went through to score the winning point and that the Cork player should therefore have been awarded a free before he scored. It was an odd and unsavoury spectacle of a team begging to be rewarded for their lack of sportsmanship. It didn't work.

Cork were back on the road to Croke Park for the chance to clinch their fourth title. The champions were on their best form in the final, setting a record that will probably never be matched by walloping their old rivals, Dublin, 2-13 to 1-2, with Kelly playing his finest game ever for the Rebels.

The historic four-in-a-row team were:

Tom Mulcahy

Willie Murphy   **Batt Thornhill**   **Din Joe Buckley**

Paddy O'Donovan   **Con Murphy**   **Alan Lotty**

Con Cottrell   **Jack Lynch**

Christy Ring   **Sean Condon**   **Jim Young**

Johnny Quirke   **Jim Morrison**   **Joe Kelly**

(Sub. Paddy Healy)

The cup was coming home – again. The train bringing the players back to Cork stopped in Blarney and they were brought the rest of the way into the city on horse-drawn coaches with the Volunteers Pipe Band parading in front of them. Over 20,000 boisterous supporters were there to greet their heroes.

A FINAL CHAPTER

Five All-Irelands in a row was beyond even this magnificent team and they bowed out in 1945, losing 2-13 to 3-2 to Tipperary. But, as so often with great teams, there was to be a glorious final chapter. Most of the four-in-a-row team were still there in 1946, and three new attackers – Mossie and Gerry O'Riordan and, confusingly, another Con Murphy – gave Cork a new impetus. Jack Lynch was still in midfield, even though he'd been suspended for part of the season for attending the rugby final trial to watch his brother-in-law John Harvey in action. It wasn't the first example of the lunacy of the Ban and it wouldn't be the last.

Clare were disposed of first, and Cork then had nine points to spare over Waterford. Limerick, who had looked to be back to their best when knocking out All-Ireland champions Tipperary in the semi-final, were the opposition in the Munster decider.

Greats face to face: Mick Mackey and Christy Ring check the toss before the 1946 Munster final in Thurles.

The Limerick defence comes under pressure in the 1946 Munster final against Cork in Thurles.

Incredibly, at thirty-four years of age and in his fifteenth season of inter-county hurling, Mick Mackey was still their key man. Sadly, time had achieved what the country's defenders had signally failed to do and halted the gallop of the Ahane man. He was completely negated by the quicker Din Joe Buckley and Cork won by 3-8 to 1-3, the goals coming from the new Con Murphy, Mossie O'Riordan and Joe Kelly. Cork then beat Galway 2-10 to 0-3 in the semi-final, and squared up to Kilkenny for the final.

The 1946 final proved to be one of the great one-man shows of hurling as Christy Ring began his transformation into a legend by ripping the Leinster champions apart as Cork won by 7-5 to 3-8. Just before half-time, Ring scored one of the greatest goals ever witnessed, taking a pass from Paddy O'Donovan seventy yards out, speeding past Kilkenny captain Jack Mulcahy, sidestepping defenders Walsh and Butler and flicking the ball past the goalkeeper from close range. It was as if he had contrived to salute the members of the first great Cork team he'd played on. But, of course, he was only getting started.

If there had been no Jack Lynch, it would have been necessary to invent him. The star of the Cork four-in-a-row team was the kind of man legends adhered to. The stories about Lynch are legion. There was the Cork county senior football final when St Nicholas were leading Clonakilty. A river ran alongside the pitch and when the ball was kicked into it with only a couple of minutes remaining, it looked as though the game would have to be abandoned. Enter Lynch, who leapt in, swam downstream after the ball, retrieved it and thus ensured that Nicks would win the title. Then there was the time he played three games in one day: a Dublin championship match for the civil service in the morning and two Railway Cup finals for Munster in the afternoon. He'd played the morning game because 'he didn't think it would be right to let his club down.

Lynch was never a man to back down, making him heroic on the pitch and principled off it. He always stood his ground. A good example, one of many, is the time he refused to attend the presentation of the 1939 Munster Championship medals because his Glen Rovers' team-mate, Jim Young, had been suspended under the Ban for going to a dance run by a rugby club.

Lynch's determination marked him out as a high-achiever in everything he turned his hand to. He had to cope with losing his mother when he was only a boy of fifteen, but he went on to study law part-time while working in the civil service, qualifying as a lawyer and eventually attaining the highest office in the land, serving as taoiseach from 1966 to 1973 and again from 1977 to 1979.

Yet there was an aura of mischief about the young Lynch as well. In a sport where the ideal icon was a son of the soil, Lynch was working class and urban. His father was a tailor, his mother a seamstress and Lynch grew up in the warren of narrow streets around Shandon Cathedral in Cork City. His childhood memories resembled those of some North of England soccer player rather than those of hurlers (like Lory Meagher, who remembered pucking the ball around the paddock). On wet days, Lynch pucked around in the cellar of his house, when it was dry he and his friends hurled in the Butter Market, scarpering from the gardaí who arrived to enforce the law against playing games on the streets, using their knowledge of the lanes to get away. Lynch was a star of that urban of teams: the Glen.

Lynch is the only player in history to win six All-Ireland senior medals in a row – his five hurling medals in six years being interrupted in 1945 when Cork won the football championship. He was a tough competitor, a tremendous athlete and went on to become the most popular Irishman since Daniel O'Connell.

It has been said about Lynch's political contemporary, Richard Nixon, that he epitomised all the hidden darkness of the American soul, revealed all that was wrong with that country's national character. The reverse is true of Lynch: he was a mirror in which the Irish people saw themselves as they would like to be – at their best.

THE GREATEST RIVALRY, PART I

Tipperary, 1949–1951

Munster Champions 1949, 1950, 1951

All-Ireland Champions 1949, 1950, 1951

Tipperary are the third member of hurling's Holy Trinity, Cork and Kilkenny being the other two. The county has a proud hurling tradition: in 1887 they became the first county to win the All-Ireland and went on to win seven of the first fifteen championships. But by the end of the 1940s they had fallen on lean times, having been eclipsed by the superb Limerick and Cork sides of the previous few decades. Before the 1949 championship started, Tipp had won just three of the previous twenty titles – a poor return for such a hurling stronghold. Worse still, in the previous three seasons they hadn't won even one match and their fortune didn't look likely to change in the near future.

Starting in 1949, however, it took Tipp just three years to equal that twenty-year haul and to re-establish the county as one of the major hurling powers. The team that achieved this feat contained some of the game's true legends: Tony Reddan gets many people's vote as the greatest goalkeeper of them all; the indomitable John Doyle was just beginning his lengthy career at corner-back; and there has probably never been a better half-back line than that of Jimmy Finn, Pat Stakelum and Tommy Doyle. And if their attack was less spectacular, it still contained wonderful players, such as the Kenny brothers from Borrisoleigh – the goal-poaching Paddy and the athletic Sean – and the supremely accurate Jimmy Kennedy. But despite putting Tipp back on the map, it is not for All-Ireland wins that this particular team will be remembered. They were part of one of the greatest sporting rivalries of all time, one of those which, like Frazier versus Ali, Borg versus McEnroe, or Kerry versus Dublin, means that the names of the contestants will be forever intertwined.

The team that they thwarted for three years in a row were a superb Cork team that included Christy Ring at the height of his powers. It's telling that when Tipp finally took their eye off the ball, that Cork side put together their own three-in-a-row. But their story will come later.

CORK'S LATE LEVELLER

Tipp's three-in-a-row story began on 29 May 1949. The opposition, almost inevitably, was Cork and the warring teams attracted a record crowd, 34,702 people, for a first-round

Jackie Power of Limerick, one of the great forwards of the 1940s, tries to break through the Tipperary defence in the 1949 Munster final at the Cork Athletic Grounds.

match in Limerick. The make-up of the two sides was very different: Cork still had some survivors from the four-in-a-row era, while Tipp's Paddy Kenny, Pat Stakelum, Michael Ryan and Phil Shanahan were only a couple of years out of minor ranks. The subs included an eighteen-year-old from Holycross named John Doyle. And those spectators who turned up to watch Tipp beat Cork in the minor curtain-raiser would have seen a prodigious centre half-back, Jimmy Finn, who within a year would be a key member of the senior team and by 1951 would be captain.

For most of the match it looked as though youth would trump age, and with only a few minutes left Tipp were 3-10 to 2-9 ahead. But Jack Lynch had other ideas and soloed through from midfield for a great goal that gave him a personal tally of 1-6 and left just a point between the sides. A solo point from another veteran, Bernie Murphy, levelled the scores right at the death. The teams left the pitch knowing they'd have to come back and do it all again.

The replay turned out to be a classic. John Doyle was brought into a reshuffled Tipperary defence and thus began one of the longest and most distinguished of all inter-county careers. This time around it was Cork who looked the better side. A Gerry O'Riordan goal gave them a 1-2 to 0-2 lead at the break, and they could have been out of sight but for one of those odd incidents that decorate the history of the Munster championship. Mossie O'Riordan sent a shot past Reddan and the *sliotha*r appeared to come back off the stanchion supporting the net before being cleared. The referee waved play on and, though some Tipperary fans insist to this day that the shot had actually hit the crossbar, it seems clear that Cork were robbed of a goal at a crucial moment.

Despite their bad luck, Cork still led by 1-5 to 0-5 deep into injury time. Five minutes of injury time had already been played and the spectators were leaving in their droves when Tipp's Jimmy Kennedy scored an equalising goal to send the match into extra time.

The different approaches taken by the teams before extra time may have significantly affected the result. It was one of the warmest days ever recorded in Ireland, but the Cork players stayed out in the burning sun. Tipperary retired to their dressing room where their exhausted and battered players seriously considered not playing the extra time. They were persuaded to fight on by a rousing speech from manager Paddy Leahy and were further revived when the Blakes of Coolquill, a well-known sporting family from the county, arrived with water in a creamery churn. Years later, Jimmy Kennedy said he could still feel the blessed coolness of that water as it was poured over him. Tipperary took the field a much fresher team. Brilliant centre half-forward Mick Ryan gave them the lead with an early goal and they held out to win 2-8 to 1-9. It really was the end of an era for Cork, as Willie Murphy, Alan Lotty and Jim Young hung up their hurleys after the game.

There had been many heroic performances on both sides, but those two games in 1949 will be forever associated with Tommy Doyle. Known as the Rubber Man because of his ability to bounce back from punishment, Doyle was a member of the famous Thurles Sarsfields club. He also excelled at boxing and idolised Joe Louis and Sugar Ray Robinson. He had won All-Ireland medals in 1937 and 1945, but four years later, at the age of thirty-four, seemed to be past his best.

In fact, Doyle was just on his way home from posting a letter to the county secretary Phil Purcell, announcing his retirement, when he bumped into selector John Joe Callanan. Callanan informed Doyle that regular corner-back Tom Purcell was ill (he sadly died of the illness), and asked Doyle if he'd like to mark Ring in the championship.

It proved an inspired decision as Doyle outplayed Ring in both games, keeping the game's greatest player scoreless for the duration of two matches, plus extra time. Ring did score a point when he switched briefly off Doyle in replay extra time, but Doyle immediately went back on him and curbed the Corkman again. It was perhaps the greatest exhibition of marking in the history of the game, made all the more commendable by the fact that Doyle played the replay with a bandage wrapped around a head wound that later required six stitches. He had sustained the injury in a clash with Ring. So confident did Doyle become, that when Ring took off his boots – always a sign that he was going to put in an extra effort – his marker quipped, 'Christy, you can leave them on. You're not going to get any points today.'

T H E   N O V E L T Y   O F   L A O I S

In the semi-final, Tipp beat Clare 1-15 to 1-7 in Limerick. Clare led by two points with fifteen minutes left, but sub. Tommy Ryan scored a great goal and a point to turn the game Tipp's way. In the provincial final they beat Limerick 1-16 to 2-10, Kennedy contributing ten points and Reddan making some great saves, though luck was on his side when a goal by veteran Jackie Power was controversially disallowed. Ironically, both starring players had come to Tipp from other counties. Kennedy, a Tipp native, had played with Dublin as recently as the 1948 All-Ireland final. He came back home at the start of the 1949 championship and went on to score a superb 2-27 from four games in Munster, 0-20 coming from frees. Reddan, from Mullagh in Galway, despaired of ever getting the nod for the Galway goalkeeper's jersey ahead of the great Sean Duggan and moved the few miles across the border to Lorrha in north Tipperary, thus qualifying to play for that county. It proved a wise move for the man who trained by striking the *sliothar* into the air and trapping it on his hurley while out ploughing the land.

As so often in that period, getting out of Munster was the most difficult part. Tipperary trounced Antrim in the semi-final and prepared for the challenge of Laois, who had shocked everyone by reaching their first All-Ireland final in thirty-four years. The novelty of the pairing drew 67,000 fans to Croker and Laois managed to stay in touch in the first-half, trailing just 1-5 to 0-3 at half-time. But Tipperary opened up in the second-half to score 2-6 without reply. Full-back Tony Brennan gave an outstanding display, showing a rare versatility for the time; when Tipp had won the 1945 final, the big man was playing full-forward. So Tipp returned home clutching the McCarthy Cup, perhaps already aware that Cork eagerly awaited the chance to turn the tables the following year.

A N A R C H Y   I N   K I L L A R N E Y

There was an inevitability about the meeting of Tipp and Cork in the 1950 Munster final, though both had had close shaves in the semi – Tipperary having three points to spare over Limerick, Cork just two over Waterford. The final was fixed for Killarney and it proved to be a nadir in the history of crowd-troubled matches, a day when the unruliness of the spectators almost directly affected the result.

The attendance for the final was given officially as 39,000. In fact, over 50,000 people watched the match that day. Gates were broken down, walls were scaled and the pitch was regularly invaded by the uncontrollable fans. It was total anarchy in Killarney and a rejoinder to those of us who imagine the 1950s as a repressed and joyless time when the citizens lived in a state of perpetual obedience. These spectators exhibited the kind of fanaticism more commonly associated with South American soccer matches. There were even a few on the pitch at the throw-in, and a Cork fan tried to strike Sean Kenny, only to be stopped by Jack Lynch.

It didn't seem to bother Tipperary who played marvellous hurling, completely outplaying Cork to take a 1-13 to 1-6 lead, with Mick Ryan and Jimmy Kennedy in unstoppable form. They were 2-17 to 2-9 ahead going into the final quarter when the Cork fans invaded the field *en masse*. It took ten minutes to clear the pitch and, with Tipp obviously rattled, the Rebels launched a fight back. Cork had cut the lead to three points with five minutes remaining and were looking more confident by the minute, but the situation on the pitch was now verging on the surreal. One of Cork's goals resulted from a ball that had gone wide being kicked back onto the pitch by their supporters.

Every Cork score was greeted by a crowd invasion, and their main target was the Tipp keeper, Reddan. Surrounded by enemy supporters, he came under a barrage of oranges (some of which he peeled and ate) and sods. He was pushed several times. On one occasion a Cork fan caught him by the jersey as he ran out to clear the ball, and on another an overcoat was thrown at him as he prepared to make a save. Jack Lynch appealed to the Cork supporters to calm down, but they paid no heed. In the end, the Cork players seemed as distracted as their opponents by the whole caper and Tipp held on grimly to win 2-17 to 3-11. Right at the end, Cork were awarded a seventy, but there were so many spectators between the referee and his umpires that a puck-out was given instead. The comment of Tipperary corner-back Mickey Byrne that it was 'dog rough' summed up the day pretty well.

The crowd trouble continued after the final whistle. Referee Bill O'Donoghue was assaulted by Cork fans and could have been seriously injured but for Ring, who rescued him and stayed by him until a garda escort arrived. Reddan had to be shepherded off the field by a group of priests who tried to disguise him with a hat and coat. However, the Cork supporters were out for the keeper's blood and it was several hours before he could be smuggled, in disguise, out of the ground. It had come far too close to being the worst day in the GAA's history, one of the few times when passion and local pride turned nasty.

After such an ordeal, an easy semi-final win over Galway must have come as a relief. Paddy Kenny's hat-trick of goals saw the champions through by seven points. Kilkenny would provide the final opposition, and with Tipp having an almost perpetual Indian Sign over their neighbours, the Munster champions went in as favourites. Kilkenny, however, had upset the odds in 1947 with a win over Cork in one of the greatest finals ever played and they had many of the same team in action. In Jimmy Langton they had one of the all-time legends of the game and they had run Tipp to four points in the League final earlier that year.

By half-time in the final it looked as though the Leinster champions were about to upset the applecart, they led 0-7 to 0-5 and would have the wind behind them in the second-half. But if there was one thing Tipperary had learned in Munster, it was how to dig deep. Kilkenny, unaccountably, froze and Tipp grabbed the opportunity with both hands, leading 0-9 to 0-8 in the closing stages. Paddy Kenny's goal a couple of minutes from the end seemed to clinch it for them, but Jimmy Kelly replied immediately in kind for Kilkenny. There were a few nervous moments, but Tipp held on to win 1-9 to 1-8. The performance of Jimmy Finn was crucial. Aged only nineteen, he outplayed Jimmy Langton for much of the match and held the great forward to just two points from play. It was a match-winning contribution. This was Tipp's first two-in-a-row since 1899. Their precursors had completed a three-in-a-row in 1900, but to emulate that Tipp would once more have to get past Cork.

THE THIRD INSTALMENT

The 1951 campaign started shakily for Tipperary when Waterford went down by only 2-10 to 1-10 in the first round, but they went on to score a comprehensive win over

Limerick in the semi-final. The champions were poised for the third instalment of what was becoming a serial between themselves and Cork. The final was played in Limerick on a scorching hot July day. The authorities were taking no chances on a repeat of the previous year's fun and games. Thousands of spectators were locked outside the gates before the match started and had to follow the match from a radio broadcast. Even allowing for the huge number of excluded spectators, the GAA raked in record receipts – twice the previous total, in fact. The exact amount? A princely £6,207. Those unfortunates locked outside missed one of the greatest games of all time, the one in

Above: *One of the greatest games of all time. Frantic defence by Cork in the 1951 Munster final against Tipperary in the Gaelic Grounds, Limerick.*

Opposite: *The greatest goalkeeper of them all, Tony Reddan, defends his lines for Tipperary against Clare in the National League in Ennis in 1956.*

which Christy Ring gave his greatest display, the likes of which had not been seen before and has not been seen since.

Tipp were two points up at half-time, 0-9 to 1-4, but Cork moved up a gear early in the second-half. Ring blasted a free to the net from forty yards, added a point from a free and a Willie John Daly point left Cork three points up in total by the end of the third-quarter. Ring was roaming the whole field, collecting possession, beating tackles, setting up attacks, taking the defence on himself. It was as if everything he had done before had been leading to this day, this game. But it wasn't enough. Any other team would have been swept aside by Ring, but Tipp, though they buckled, did not break. Reddan was as dependable as ever in goals, and the full-back line of Mickey 'The Rattler' Byrne, Tony Brennan and John Doyle withstood ferocious pressure.

The match turned back their way when Mick Ryan was switched from centre half-forward to midfield. Ryan thundered into the game and started the move that ended with his namesake, Ned Ryan, scoring the equalising goal. Sonny Maher and Willie John Daly then swopped points before Tipp looked to have scored the winning goal, Sonny Maher sweeping the ball home into the net from close range. Ring was in no mood to be denied, however, and he flung off his boots and socks – a gesture much beloved of hurlers for many years – before scoring two frees, leaving just one point between the sides. But it was Tipp who had the last word, Paddy Kenny angling a shot over the bar to see them home by 2-11 to 2-9. The great Tipperary team had given their finest performance. It seemed as though they could take anything Cork threw at them.

BIG, EXUBERANT AND PHYSICAL

There would be new opposition in the 1951 All-Ireland final: Wexford. The Slaneysiders had not appeared in a decider since 1918, and it had been forty-one years since they had won the championship. But there was a buzz around their current team, a big, exuberant, physical side containing players of the calibre of Nicky Rackard, his brothers Bobby and Billy, Nick O'Donnell and Tim Flood, all of whom would become legends over the course of the next few years.

The 70,000 spectators who descended on Croke Park on All-Ireland day were greeted by the odd sight of Tipperary wearing blue and Wexford wearing green because the colour clash between the two counties necessitated the donning of provincial colours. Wexford lived up to their advance billing in the first-quarter when they jumped into a five-point lead, bagging their first goal when the towering Nicky Rackard bundled Reddan, the *sliothar* and anyone else nearby into the net. It was like a red rag to the Tipp defence and they hit the Wexford attack hard after that. By half-time the champions had recovered to lead by a goal. It still looked too close to call, but the second-half was a parade for the champions with Wexford tiring badly and their keeper, Ray Brennan, making a litany of errors. At the other end, the incomparable Reddan made a string of saves to rub salt in the wound. Tipperary cruised home by 7-7 to 3-9.

It had been another tremendous year for Tipperary and they looked a good bet to equal Cork's four-in-a-row record. (In the next chapter we'll examine how Cork managed to put paid to that aspiration.)

The 1951 Tipp team that completed the three-in-a-row were:

Tony Reddan

Mickey Byrne   **Tony Brennan**   **John Doyle**

Jimmy Finn   **Pat Stakelum**   **Tommy Doyle**

Phil Shanahan   **John Hough**

Ned Ryan   **Mick Ryan**   **Timmy Ryan**

Paddy Kenny   **Sonny Maher**   **Seamus Bannon**

(Sub. Sean Kenny)

I never saw John Doyle in action. Well, not in action on the pitch anyway. In the summer of 2000, I was in the press box in Semple Stadium talking to another journalist when a burly, black-suited man hurtled towards us. He informed my fellow journalist that he took grave exception to being described as a gorilla in that morning's newspaper. John Doyle was not a happy man.

'Oh, you're John Doyle,' said my colleague. 'I didn't call you a gorilla. I quoted Tony Wall as saying it. He meant it as a compliment.'

'Tony Wall would know better than to say that about me,' retorted Doyle. 'You wrote it. Take it back, or don't come to Thurles again.'

As it happens, the journalist, Dermot Crowe of the *Sunday Independent*, did not take it back. He's a Clareman, and Claremen these days don't tend to back away from Tipperarymen. Nonetheless, Doyle had certainly left an impression on us, although there wasn't any need for him to take the comment so much to heart. It seemed beneath a man of his status in the game. Yet you had to admire a man of nearly seventy who was still that passionate and who still cut an imposing, almost fearsome figure.

That was always the way with John Doyle. You couldn't be indifferent to him. No player was worshipped to such an extent by his own fans nor so resolutely damned by those from other counties. The first defender to become a big star, Doyle was undoubtedly the finest corner-back yet seen, but his name was also a by-word for a toughness that teetered on the edge of legality. In a western movie, John Doyle would have been played by Robert Ryan, wearing a black hat.

For all that, it would be foolish to play down Doyle's hurling ability. Over six-feet tall and weighing thirteen-and-a-half stone at his peak, he was nonetheless very quick over short distances and his underestimated skill enabled him to make clearances in the tightest of situations. When he decided to burst through a pack of attackers, there was no stopping him. He might have dished out punishment, but he could take it too and never complained. His was the uncomplicated creed of the genuine hard man. 'We lived in a tougher and harder school,' he once said.

Doyle won eight All-Ireland medals, picking them up in three different decades. He first caught the eye as a young corner-back on that 1949–1951 Tipperary team. He could easily have retired in the 1950s due to the pressure of the combined demands of running a large family farm and playing inter-county hurling, but John Doyle wasn't a quitter and he stuck at it. His performance at left half-back in the 1958 All-Ireland semi-final against Kilkenny was one of the great individual displays of the decade.

Most of all though, John Doyle will ever be associated with Hell's Kitchen, the ruthless full-back line he made up along with Mick Maher and Kieran Carey in the 1960s. Justin McCarthy's wry comment that 'no one scored 3-5 off Hell's Kitchen and lived', when he heard that Eamon Cregan had taken the full-back line to the cleaners in 1966, shows the reputation that the trio enjoyed.

Doyle is rumoured to have invented the Hell's Kitchen nickname himself. It would figure. The man's off-the-field pronouncements were as uncompromising as his hurling. When it was put to him in 1965 that a younger Cork team would run Tipp off the field, Doyle replied, 'They can do the running, and we'll do the hurling.' In his own way, John Doyle was as much of a legend as Ring and Mackey. Great drama, after all, needs both heroes and villains.

THE GREATEST RIVALRY, PART II

Cork, 1952–1956

Munster Champions 1952, 1953, 1954, 1956

All-Ireland Champions 1952, 1953, 1954

For three years in a row, from 1949 to 1951, Cork had come up just short against Tipperary on Munster final days. Even with Ring at full throttle they seemed to be lacking the little bit extra that would return them to the top of the provincial pile. By 1952, Cork had an extra motivating factor because they realised that if Tipperary got past them, they'd almost certainly make it four All-Irelands in a row and thereby take the gloss off the record set by the Rebel side of the 1940s. Between 1949 and 1954 Cork and Tipp enjoyed an annual date, and every year the winner of their tussle went on to win the All-Ireland. Never have two hurling teams been so completely locked in their own one-to-one battle, so completely superior to every other team in the country.

In 1952, even with Cork in their way, Tipp looked a good bet for the championship – even more so after they won the National League. There was an experimental look about a Cork team with several championship débutants. But the difference between the aristocrats of hurling – Cork, Kilkenny and Tipperary – and the pretenders is that the traditional powers can constantly produce new players of the highest quality. As the old saying goes, 'Cork are like the mushroom, they can come up overnight.'

Nonetheless, the Cork line-up was fresh-faced and inexperienced, with seven newcomers and a lot to prove. The three wonder-kids of the 1940s who might have been expected to be at their peak now had all quit the game: Joe Kelly had emigrated, while Mick Kennefick and Sean Condon had had potentially legendary careers cut short by injury. Among the new crop of young players were John Lyons, one of the outstanding full-backs of his era, the excellent corner-back Tony O'Shaughnessy who went on to give an exhibition in the 1954 All-Ireland final, and a couple of new forwards – Paddy Barry from the Sarsfields club in Glanmire, and his fellow east Corkman, Willie John Daly of Carrigtwohill. This brilliant duo proved to be the ideal foils for Christy Ring, now in his thirties but seeming to improve with each passing year.

The biggest problem for this Cork team was in the goalkeeping department. First-choice keeper Mick Cashman withdrew from the panel, his deputy Jim Cotter was ill and the next in line, Sean Carroll, fell foul of the GAA ban on attending foreign games. So it looked like desperation when Cork turned to Dave Creedon of Glen Rovers. Creedon had been sub. goalie on the four-in-a-row team a decade previously, but he had never broken into the championship side. In fact, he had recently retired from the game altogether, but agreed to don the jersey one last time for his county. Creedon's selection turned out to be an inadvertent masterstroke. The Glen man was one of the key members of the 1952–1954 team, and his record of conceding just one goal in three consecutive All-Ireland finals hasn't been rivalled since.

Limerick put Cork under pressure in the Munster semi-final of 1952 in Thurles. In their next game, Cork destroyed Tipperary's hopes of four All-Irelands in a row.

Cork had an easy win over Limerick in the 1952 Munster semi-final, 6-6 to 2-4, but it looked like the same old story in the provincial final when they conceded a soft goal to Tipp in the third minute. They managed to rally and trailed only 2-5 to 0-5 at half-time after playing against a strong wind. Two great Reddan saves prevented goals from Ring and kept Tipp ahead in the second-half. By the final quarter the favourites still had four points to spare after points from Ring and Gerard Murphy.

Then came the crucial score. Mossie O'Riordan, bursting through the Tipp defence, was fouled but carried on to fire in a shot that Liam Dowling steered into the net. Tipp's

This isn't why they called him Ringy. Christy Ring kisses the ring of the Archbishop of Cashel, Most Rev. Dr Kinane, prior to the 1953 All-Ireland final between Cork and Galway. The mood of Christian charity didn't last long!

protests to the referee that O'Riordan should have been awarded a free came to nought. It seems that the score would have been ruled out but for the intervention of Ring, whose words prompted the umpire to raise the green flag and the referee to forget the letter of the law. There was still a point in it, but the goal seemed to crush the champions' spirit. Ring fired over three points in a row and Sean O'Brien landed a huge free. A late Gerry Doyle shot for Tipp flew inches over the crossbar and it was all over: Cork had won by 1-11 to 2-7, preventing Tipp from achieving the four-in-a-row. Ring, who'd been heroic in adversity, was shouldered off the field with blood streaming down his face and a bandage around his head thanks to a belt from a stray hurley in the thick of the battle.

As had happened in 1944, Cork again found Galway to be tricky opposition in the All-Ireland semi-final and scraped through by two points, 1-5 to 0-6, with a soft goal from Josie Hartnett and two late points by Joe Twomey and Ring proving vital. Great Galway midfielder Joe Salmon, who would later play with Glen Rovers, had almost beaten Cork on his own. The Munster champions would next face old rivals and perennial final-losers Dublin in the final.

The team from the capital included two Corkmen, Con Murphy and Sean Cronin. Murphy was the Bride Rovers player who had played for his home county in the 1946 and 1947 finals. Dublin had a slight edge in the first-half, with dual star Des Ferguson doing very well on Ring, and they would have led at half-time but for a great save by Creedon from a Tony Herbert shot. Cork broke upfield straight away and a Liam Dowling goal left them 1-5 to 0-5 up at the break. The second-half, however, was a victory procession. Ring and Barry shot three points each and Dowling scored another goal. Dublin failed to muster a response and Cork won 2-14 to 0-7.

DEFENDING CHAMPIONS

Cork's defence of the crown started in 1953 with an unexpectedly tough game against a Clare side that had put ten goals past Limerick in their opening match. Cork were still expected to win easily, but led by only four points at half-time. In a thrilling second-half two goals from Jackie Greene left the sides level going into the closing stages. A shock result looked on until Hartnett sent a ferocious twenty-five-yard drive to the net and Daly followed up with a point. The estimable Creedon prevented a frantic finish by superbly turning a Jimmy Smith shot over the bar. Cork were through, but they hadn't heard the last of Mister Smith.

Tipperary, naturally, were waiting in the Munster final. Around 43,000 fans saw the game in Limerick, with locked-out Cork fans breaking down a gate to get in. Tipp had the wind behind them in the first-half, but only led by four points, 1-8 to 1-4, after Ring scored a typical goal from a twenty-one-yard free. Pat Stakelum put Tipp five points clear, but Tipp made a crucial mistake when switching Jimmy Finn off Josie Hartnett to mark Ring. A rejuvenated Hartnett fired in a great shot that Reddan could only parry, and Liam Dowling flashed the rebound into the net. Ring levelled with a pointed free and the key moment came when he stopped a Paddy Kenny twenty-one-yard free on his own line and cleared upfield, setting in motion a series of moves that ended with Terry Kelly scoring the clinching goal for a delighted Cork. Ring ended the day with 1-8 to his credit.

It was one of the most impressive Munster final performances in years, and Cork came out of it as hot favourites for the All-Ireland final against Galway, who had shocked Kilkenny in the semi-final. All the same, the final drew a record crowd of 71,195 whose reward was to witness probably the dirtiest decider ever played. Galway seemed to have decided that the physical route was the one to take against Cork and against Ring, in particular. The Galway captain, Mickey Burke, was detailed to mark Cork's star player and he handed out some harsh treatment, while the partisan Galway crowd booed Ring

The Cork team that took on Galway in the 1953 All-Ireland final at Croke Park and in the afters at the Gresham Hotel and Barry's Hotel.

Christy Ring with the Liam McCarthy Cup after the famously dirty 1953 All-Ireland final against Galway.

every time he got possession. There was little constructive play in the game. Galway fell five points behind in the first twenty minutes with Ring and Hartnett finding the net. Cork led by 2-1 to 0-3 at half-time, but in the second-half the Tribesmen dominated. This was despite the fact that Burke was badly injured midway through that period. In fact, though there was much pussyfooting about it at the time, Ring had put up with enough of Burke's attentions and punched him in the jaw. The Cork star had moved out to midfield to get rid of the Galway captain, but found his shadow continuing to dog him. Burke suffered a damaged jaw and broken teeth and probably should have gone off, but he continued to follow Ring, presumably hoping for a chance of revenge. This upset the balance of the Galway defence at a crucial time.

Meanwhile, the Cork full-back line of Gerry O'Riordan, John Lyons and Tony O'Shaughnessy were playing brilliantly under pressure as the favourites held on to a one-point lead in the dying stages during one of the longest scoreless periods in modern final history. This time it was the gritty Willie John Daly who threw off his boots and put Cork two points clear. Galway's John Killeen brought the deficit back to the minimum going into injury time and it was still anyone's game. An injury-time goal from Tom O'Sullivan saw Cork through by 3-3 to 0-8 and decided an unprecedentedly bitter battle.

The ill feeling didn't stop there. That night, as the Cork team celebrated their victory in the Gresham Hotel, some of the Galway players arrived seeking revenge. Ring was carrying the Cup out of the ballroom when he was hit in the face by a Galway player and knocked down the steps, and players on both sides got involved in the ensuing fight. Order was soon restored but, interestingly, the president of the GAA, Vincent O'Donoghue, had witnessed the whole affair. Despite this the GAA authorities never took any action over the incident.

Ring's nemesis: Art Foley, the Wexford goalkeeper, clears in the 1956 All-Ireland final against Cork. Foley's late save from Ring put the kibosh on the Glen man's hopes of a ninth All-Ireland medal.

Above: *Nicky English is sent tumbling to the ground in the unsavoury 1989 Munster final, which Tipperary won by 0-26 to 2-8 against Waterford.*

Below: *Ciaran Carey of Limerick, one of the finest hurlers of the 1990s. His destruction by PJ O'Connell in the 1995 Munster final paved the way for Clare's historic win.*

Above: *John Leahy (Number Nine) was one of Tipp's stars in the 1990s. Here he shows typical commitment against Derek Barrett of Cork. Notice that Leahy is making sure no one gets away with his hurley after the game.*

Below: *Michael Cleary had an outstanding year in 1991. Here the graceful wing-forward breaks through the Kilkenny defence in the All-Ireland final.*

Above: *A tired but happy Tipperary team bring the Liam McCarthy Cup into Thurles in 1989.*

Below: *Two of the hardiest competitors in the game: John Power of Kilkenny heads goalwards pursued by Tipp's Bobby Ryan in the 1991 All-Ireland final.*

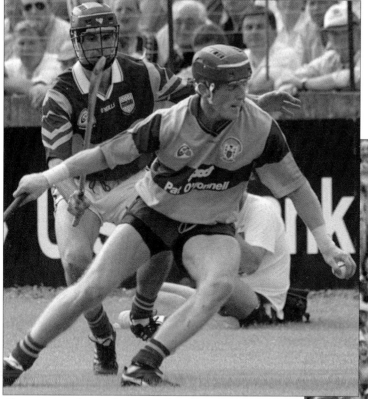

Above: *Brian Lohan evades Kevin Tucker of Tipperary in the 1997 Munster final. 'The day,' Ger Loughnane said, 'Clare earned respect.'*

Right: *English's ducks prepare to drown, but Tipp are rescued by a Fox: Nicky English has just kicked the equalising point in the 1991 Munster final against Cork, but the umpires are about to agree with Cork keeper Ger Cunningham and wave it wide.*

Above: *Clare hunting in packs, as always, against Tipperary. Anthony Daly and Ollie Baker are typically to the fore.*

Right: *PJ O'Connell bursts through the tackle of Offaly centre half-back Hubert Rigney in the 1995 All-Ireland final.*

Michael Ryan of Tipperary tries to escape the attentions
of Tomas Mulcahy in the 1991 Munster final.

And there were more shenanigans the next morning as the Cork players ate breakfast in Barry's Hotel. Seven Galway players stormed into the dining room and once more Ring received a punch. This time he was surrounded by Glen club-mates who hit back, causing the Galway players to flee into a nearby room and lock the door behind them. Enter Jim Barry, with a chair, to try and break the door down. Hotel management somehow succeeded in getting the Cork players back to their rooms so the Galway mob could leave the hotel unmolested. An attempt later that day by the same group of Galway players to start a row with Cork players outside the hotel was foiled by the arrival of a garda. You can only imagine the furore on 'Liveline', 'Sportscall' and the like if it happened today, but at the time the GAA seemed reluctant to take action.

The Galway County Board, for a start, was not too fussed about the attack on Ring, commenting that 'the steps where the incidents occurred were well-carpeted ones.' The board made a further meal of it by striking a special medal to award their clobbered captain. The inscription read: 'For courage, endurance of pain, chivalry and outstanding self-restraint.' The threat by Galway GAA fans to burn copies of the *Cork Examiner* in Eyre Square fortunately never came to fruition. It had been a bizarre episode all round.

More attendance records tumbled in 1954 as Cork and Tipperary met in another Munster final in Limerick in front of a crowd of 52,499. Tipp led by six points at half-time but it didn't seem to be enough as they'd played with a strong wind at their backs. Nevertheless they still led by a point as the match moved into injury time, only to be betrayed by the unthinkable: a mistake by Tony Reddan. Ring, although swarmed by three players, got in a speculative cross, the great keeper fumbled and Paddy Barry was in like a flash to finish to the net. A point by Ring followed, and when the final whistle blew Cork were still on course for a three-in-a-row. Once more, Ring had been the difference between the teams, scoring a great goal from a twenty-one-yard free early in the second-half.

All the same, Tipperary were entitled to feel that they had been robbed, as Cork had been in 1949. Midway through the second-half, Seamus Bannon had taken on the Cork defence single-handedly and buried the ball in the net. It would have been one of the great Munster final goals had it been allowed. A crafty Cork defender had thrown a hurley in the general direction of Bannon, causing the referee to blow for a free-in just before the goal was scored. The advantage rule that had benefitted Liam Dowling and Cork two years previously didn't seem to apply to Tipperary. The memory rankled for a long time.

A much more subdued Galway were overwhelmed 4-13 to 2-1 in the All-Ireland semi-final, and the stage was set for what was one of the most eagerly anticipated All-Ireland finals of all time. The charismatic giants from Wexford had reached their second final in three years and this time they looked well capable of winning.

Perhaps no team and no player has ever exhibited the awesome pre-final form that Wexford and full-forward Nicky Rackard did that year. Rackard was a different type of forward from Ring. Ferociously strong and with one of the hardest shots in the history of hurling, he did not have the Corkman's skill but on his day he looked unstoppable – like Sonny Liston in his boxing heyday. In the Leinster final he had scored 5-4, and in the All-Ireland semi-final against Antrim he had notched up 7-7. In the three championship games they had played, Wexford had scored 25-33 in total and had conceded just 3-14. On the day, 84,000 fans crammed into Croke Park for what looked sure to be a festival of scoring: a shooting match between Rackard and Ring.

But that wasn't how it turned out at all. Defences were on top all day and John Lyons, unspectacular but massively composed and intelligent, got the better of Rackard. Ring, too, was well marked as Wexford led 1-3 to 0-5 at half-time thanks to a Tom Ryan goal. Then came a terrible blow for the Slaneysiders when Nick O'Donnell, arguably the finest full-back ever, broke his collar bone in a collision with Ring six minutes after the break. The defensive reshuffle saw Bobby Rackard moved to full-back where he played out of his skin as Wexford moved four points clear, coming into the last quarter with two points from the flying Tim Flood and one from Padge Kehoe, putting them 1-6 to 0-5 ahead.

Limerick clear their lines in the 1956 Munster final against Cork. Three goals in four minutes by Christy Ring eventually turned the tide for the Rebels.

But the game was far from over. With O'Shaughnessy clearing everything at the back, Cork slowly got back on top and began to grind Wexford down. Ring hit the target and then Vincie Twomey rallied the side by charging up from half-back to land a wonderful point – a rarity for a half-back in those days of more rigid positions. But they were still two points down with four minutes left when Wexford keeper Art Foley made an ill-judged sortie off his line and Johnny Clifford, who'd been a minor just three years before, beat him and knocked the ball into the empty net. Two late points gave Cork a 1-9 to 1-6 win and made Ring the first player to win eight All-Ireland medals.

The Cork team that completed the three-in-a-row were:

Dave Creedon

Gerry O'Riordan   **John Lyons**   **Tony O'Shaughnessy**

Matt Fouhy   **Vincie Twomey**   **Derry Hayes**

Gerry Murphy   **Willie Moore**

Willie John Daly   **Josie Hartnett**   **Christy Ring**

Johnny Clifford   **Eamonn Goulding**   **Paddy Barry**

(Sub. Tom O'Sullivan)

The four-in-a-row, however, was beyond this team, too. Amazingly, they were defeated by Clare in the first round of the 1955 Munster Championship. Clare led 2-5 to 1-0 after twenty minutes, with two goals from Jackie Greene, and though Cork levelled in the closing stages, a Jimmy Smith point gave the Banner a famous victory.

Then it seemed to be back to business as usual in 1956. In the Munster semi-final Cork overturned Tipperary's eleven-point half-time lead, with Ring yet again outstanding under pressure. Despite Cork's spirited play, Tipperary did seem to have been snookered out of a win by the referee. At 1-11 to 2-6 down, they engineered what would have been a winning goal for Paddy Kenny. Once more, a relatively useless free-in was awarded; somebody up there obviously had it in for Tipp. For their part, a huge gamble by the Cork management had paid dividends. Pat Healy, who had played in the minor game beforehand, was brought on in the senior final and outplayed no less an opponent than John Doyle, scoring a point himself and setting up two for the ubiquitous Ring. Cork were on their way again.

In the Munster final provincial champions Limerick, trained by Mick Mackey, were leading 2-5 to 1-3 in the final quarter when Ring provided yet more proof that he was less a hurler and more an irresistible force of nature. In an astounding four-minute spell he scored three goals, setting Cork up for a 5-5 to 3-5 win. It was almost as though Ring intended the hat-trick to display the full repertoire of his talents: the first was handpassed to the net as he fell, the second was a fierce drive from twenty-five yards, and the third a solo effort that involved beating several defenders

The Cork players line up before the 1956 All-Ireland final against Wexford.

Beauty and the Best: Christy Ring meets the American actress Jean Seberg, best-known for her starring role in Jean-Luc Godard's classic À Bout De Souffle *(1960), at the Cork Film Festival in September 1959.*

Wexford would once again be Cork's opponents in the All-Ireland final, but the day of reckoning had to be postponed for three weeks because of a polio outbreak in Munster. This would be a different Wexford team from the one Cork had faced two years previously. This time they went in as champions, having defeated Galway in the 1955 final, and they had gained in *nous* and confidence since 1954. Such was the interest in the game that two funerals in Wexford that weekend had to be postponed because the hearses were transporting spectators to the game. The death-defying Wexford fans were rewarded with an unforgettable game of hurling.

By the twenty-fifth minute Wexford were 1-6 to 0-2 up, thanks to a goal from Padge Kehoe, a goalline clearance by Mick Morrissey and a last-ditch tackle by Bobby Rackard on Ring. Early in the second-half, however, Cork stormed back to take the lead with a goal from a Ring twenty-one-yard free, and one from Barry after a forty-yard solo run. The decisive moment arrived when Wexford had gone two points clear. Ring burst through the defence and fired in a shot, but it was saved by Foley. Ring continued his run and shook hands with Foley. Within a few seconds, Nicky Rackard scored a goal at the other end and the men from Wexford had gained revenge for 1954. They had beaten Cork 2-14 to 2-8, and Ring was never again to come so close to All-Ireland glory. Bobby Rackard and Nick O'Donnell, who had both done so much to frustrate his intentions on the day, carried the great man off the field on their shoulders. Ring would play on with Cork until he was forty-four, but his halcyon days had just ended.

He was hurling's Shakespeare, its Pele, its Mozart. He came as close to perfection as any sportsman can. Those of us who never saw him play can only feel deeply jealous of those who did because it's unlikely that there'll ever be a hurler, a phenomenon like Christy Ring ever again. Sometimes it's difficult to think of Ring as a player who took to the field Sunday after Sunday with twenty-nine others. The words 'Christy Ring' seem more connected to legend than to the prosaic reality of the pitch, as if he were a figure from some heroic tale of yore whose impossible deeds exist only in the storyteller's mind. He seemed an anachronism – a reincarnation of Cúchulainn for the modern age. But Christy Ring was real all right.

There was once a young boy whose father died when he was little. He grew up in the east Cork village of Cloyne and spent his evenings tirelessly pucking around the back garden, near the pitch that is now fronted by a statue of himself. He grew up to be a man who moved like a dancer, was as strong as a bull, quick as a top-class sprinter and wielded the *camán* like a sorcerer. Ring scored three goals in four minutes in the 1956 Munster final, he beat five Kilkenny players to score the greatest All-Ireland final goal in 1946, and in the 1953 Munster final he scored an equalising point and was back on his own goalline quickly enough to stop a twenty-one-yard free. In almost every game he played, he did something that the crowd would talk about for weeks afterwards. There's a tendency in these iconoclastic times to belittle the cult of The Greatest, to question if mythic figures were everything they're cracked up to be. Yet ask anyone who saw Ring if he was *really* that good and they'll answer without hesitation, 'Yes, and more.'

Ring had a single-minded devotion to the game that was truly obsessive. He practiced continually, every day of the year. Even on Christmas Day he would spend hours outside in the freezing cold, pucking the ball around, lofting it high in the air and trapping it when it came down. Before the 1953 Munster final his friend and future biographer, Val Dorgan – the Boswell to Ring's Johnson – visited him in Limerick's Railway Hotel where the Cork team were staying. Ring had unscrewed one of the brass knobs from the bedpost and was hopping it on his hurley. It was as if he wanted to discover the secret of hurling, to find out just how good a man could be.

Like all geniuses, Ring was a complex character and was aware of how different he was from other people. When chided once for the satisfaction he took in describing one of his legendary scores, he replied, 'Modesty is not saying you're no good when you know you are. It's knowing where you stand.' Ring was a man who always knew where he stood.

Although eulogised by popular opinion, he was no angel. Mickey Burke of Galway was concussed by a blow during the All-Ireland final in 1953, and Tom Moloughney of Tipperary had to get twelve stitches after receiving a belt in 1961 that almost certainly came from Ring. Breandán O hEithir once described Ring's extreme competitiveness as 'repellent'. The man himself commented that there were people in Cork who thought he was let out of a mental institution to play at the weekends. That was a gross exaggeration, of course, but the intensity of Ring's focus did have something almost demonic about it. Yet he was not cynical, merely striving for the sublime. And he achieved it. His name is synonymous with excellence in hurling and generations who never saw him play still accept him as the personification of brilliance with a hurley.

Off the pitch, Ring was a shy man, but in the company of friends he would often sing one of the many ballads written about him. He was good company and a good friend to those who knew him. And he was a religious man, lighting a candle in church before big games, hurrying back to evening devotions after Munster finals. Ring's extraordinary life was cut short when, in 1979, at the age of fifty-eight, he suffered a fatal heart attack in Cork City. A giant had fallen. Jack Lynch, his old team-mate, was so upset that some observers believe it caused the taoiseach's resignation soon thereafter. Christy Ring made an impact, in life and in death, like no other Irish sportsman ever has or ever will. He won eight All-Ireland medals, nine Munsters and fourteen Cork championships with the great Glen Rovers, the city club he joined in 1941 after a falling-out with Cloyne. Ring became one of their own in the Glen. A genius belongs to everybody.

C H A P T E R   F I V E

THE OUTSIDERS

Waterford, 1957–1963

Munster Champions 1957, 1959, 1963

All-Ireland Champions 1959

In Munster hurling the Big Two have always been Tipperary and Cork. Between 1940 and 1989, for example, they won forty of the fifty provincial titles on offer. In other sports, such monotonous dominance might lead to the game dwindling away among the lesser powers. Limerick, Clare and Waterford could be excused if they gave it up as a bad job and resigned themselves to eternal apprentice status. Instead, the hegemony of Cork and Tipp has made their provincial compatriots work harder, and has made those moments when the outsiders broke through all the sweeter.

Witness Clare's joy in 1995 when they bridged a sixty-three-year gap by beating Limerick in the Munster final, before adding two more Munster titles to their tally in the following three years. And remember the Limerick apotheosis of 1973 when they ended a fallow eighteen-year spell by beating Tipperary. The roars from the county when the final whistle blew could nearly be heard in Dublin. And then there's Waterford, arguably the least successful of the Munster hurling counties. Two years will ever be held sacred by their hurling fans – 1948 and 1959 – for those were the years they won their only All-Ireland senior titles. Traditionally, the first win is the landmark one, the special victory, the pre-eminent one in local folklore. But it wasn't that way with Waterford and 1948.

The reason for this was that their brilliant team of the late 1950s and early 1960s played their big games against Kilkenny, Waterford's neighbours and a county so similar that its massive success almost stands as a rebuke to the boys next door. To beat Kilkenny at their own game was sweet victory indeed. So while the 1948 final win over Dublin was indeed an historic one, the victory over Kilkenny in the feverishly exciting final of 1959 is the one we celebrate here. Like the Limerick team of the 1930s, Waterford were probably worth another couple of titles, but that just makes the one they did win all the more precious.

John Keane of Mount Sion was the link between 1948 and 1959. Had he played with a stronger county he might well be a household name, like Ring or Mackey. As it is, the cognoscenti still number him among the finest half-dozen hurlers ever to play the game. In 1948, he was centre half-forward. By 1957, when Waterford was on the rise again, he was team trainer.

Waterford were the polar opposite of the Wexford team of the time, those huge men who liked to carry the ball and use their strength to go straight down the middle. By contrast, the Waterford men were light, quick and skilful. They kept the ball moving first-time constantly and used the wings intelligently, and what they lacked in strength they compensated for with pace. No one was quicker than their captain, Frankie Walsh. He hailed from the Mount Sion club in Waterford City and played at left half-forward for his county.

Waterford's Seamus Power shows typical Decies determination as he tangles with Cork's Jimmy Brohan in the 1957 Munster final, which was won by his team. Mick Cashman looks on.

All the major Waterford stars, with just one exception, came from Mount Sion, the marvellous city club that won nine county titles in a row between 1957 and 1965. Centre half-back Martin Óg Morrissey, the midfield pairing of Seamus Power and Walsh's brother-in-law, Phil Grimes, who had been a teenage member of the 1948 team but had emigrated to the United States before they won Munster and All-Ireland titles, plus wing-forward Larry Guinan all played their hurling for a club as vital to the county's success as Ahane had been for Limerick, or Glen Rovers had been for Cork. Like the Glen, Mount Sion was an urban club from a working-class area near the heart of the city, in this case the narrow streets clustered around the hill near the county GAA ground, Walsh Park. In Waterford, Mount Sion was given the picturesque name, Top of the Roads.

The Waterford team that beat Kilkenny in the 1959 All-Ireland hurling final.

Ned Power soars into the air to deny a swinging Christy Ring in the 1959 Munster final between Waterford and Cork. Waterford won 3-9 to 2-9 and were on their way to the All-Ireland title.

The exception on the team was Tom Cheasty who played for Ballyduff club and was a centre half-forward who didn't fit the mould of the typical Waterford hurler. Cheasty was physically powerful, technically unorthodox and his speciality was barrelling right through the centre of the opposition defence. In other words, he was just the kind of foil the likes of Walsh and Guinan needed.

SNUBBING EXPECTATIONS

In 1957 Waterford announced their return to form with a string of unexpected victories. They beat Limerick by two points in the Munster semi-final and then shocked everyone by overcoming Cork 1-11 to 1-6 in the Munster final; Cork were playing without the injured Christy Ring. Waterford really should have gone on to win the All-Ireland that year. They led Kilkenny by six points with only fifteen minutes left, but were caught at the post and beaten 4-10 to 3-12, Grimes just missing a difficult last-minute free to draw the game. The following year they were hammered by Tipperary in the Munster final and murmurs about one-season wonders could be heard.

And so to 1959. Waterford faced unusual opposition in the first round in the form of blow-ins from Connacht: Galway. They had been drafted into the Munster Championship in the hopes that it would improve their hurling. Their 7-11 to 0-8 defeat wasn't much of a débutant outing, and it presaged a terrible future for the Galway team – over the next

Waterford and Tipperary dominated hurling between 1957 and 1963. Here, Cork keeper Mick Cashman, whose nephews Tom and Jim went on to win All-Ireland medals in the 1970s, 1980s and 1990s, advances to clear the ball in the 1961 Munster senior final in Limerick, the match in which someone or other, who may or may not have been Christy Ring, cleaved Tom Moloughney.

ten years they would win just one game and as often as not they were beaten comprehensively. After a mauling by Cork in 1968, they retreated to Connacht licking their many wounds, preferring to take their chances in the All-Ireland semi-finals from then on. All-Ireland champions Tipperary were favourites to win the Munster semi-final and when they opted to play against the wind in the first-half it put Waterford under pressure to build a decent lead. After one of the most incredible halves in the history of hurling, Waterford had done just that and led by 8-2 to no score, Larry Guinan having scored three goals and Charlie Ware two. Tipperary were unable to get to the *sliothar* as the speedy Waterford attackers cut them open at every opportunity. A shellshocked Tipperary made little headway in the second-half and Waterford were 9-3 to 3-4 winners. Cork once more awaited them in the Munster final, but this time the Rebels had Ring back on board and were champing at the bit to clash ash with Waterford again.

SCALING THE HEIGHTS

Ring was getting on in years by this stage, but it was still a brilliant performance by young corner-back Joe Harney to mark him out of the game as Waterford won by 3-9 to 2-9. It would be Kilkenny who would once again stand between Waterford and the Cup, but with the experience of the previous two years behind them, Waterford looked a better bet this time.

It was one of the great All-Ireland finals. Waterford led by five points at the break and Cheasty won a memorable point right at the start of the second-half, bullocking past five Kilkenny players to score. But the downside of Waterford's love of pure hurling was that they never closed down games as they should have and that went against them this time. Two goals from corner-forward Tommy O'Connell put Kilkenny a goal ahead just one minute from time. Then Waterford's Seamus Power wrote his name in the county's history books. The midfielder collected a pass from Larry Guinan forty yards out and bore down on the goal, firing in a shot that full-back Jim 'Link' Walsh deflected past his namesake, Ollie. The final whistle blew and the scoreline was Waterford 1-17, Kilkenny 5-5: a draw.

The replay four weeks later began terribly for Waterford and they trailed by 1-4 to 0-1 after only twelve minutes. Then Mick Flannelly, another Mount Sion man, scored a great goal. Tom Cunningham added a second with a brilliant overhead pull and Cheasty also goaled. By half-time the Munster champions were 3-5 to 1-8 ahead. This time there would be no mistake. With Joe Harney and Austin Flynn excelling in the full-back line, Kilkenny scored only two points in the second-half, both coming from a minor called Eddie Keher. Waterford, on the other hand, were inspired and pulled away in the final quarter, with Walsh and Cheasty leading the way. They won in some style, 3-12 to 1-10.

Ned Power

Joe Harney   **Austin Flynn**   **John Barron**

Mick Lacey   **Martin Óg Morrissey**   **Jackie Condon**

Seamus Power   **Phil Grimes**

Mick Flannelly   **Tom Cheasty**   **Frankie Walsh**

Larry Guinan   **Tom Cunningham**   **John Kiely**

(Subs Michael O'Connor, Donal Whelan)

Hurling's Mount Everest having been attained and their flag firmly placed, Waterford never again seemed motivated to reach such heights. At least not until 1963 when an ageing team enjoyed a significant last hurrah, defeating the apparently invincible three-in-a-row hopefuls Tipperary in the Munster final, 0-11 to 0-8. The accurate free-taking of the veteran Phil Grimes made the vital difference between the teams.

END OF AN ERA

Inevitably, Kilkenny were the opposition in the 1963 All-Ireland final and also inevitably it was a classic, with thirty-five scores in sixty minutes. Waterford led by 1-4 to 0-2 after thirteen minutes before mistakes by the normally brilliant Ned Power gifted goals to Tom Walsh and Tom Murphy. A shaken Waterford trailed 3-6 to 1-5 at half-time and Walsh scored another Kilkenny goal after the restart.

The fierce local rivalry that animated the clashes between Waterford and Kilkenny is evident in this shot from the 1963 All-Ireland final.

But Waterford were not going to lie down in front of their neighbours and Seamus Power and Mick Flannelly both found the net. In a frantic finish, Flannelly had another goal and Power forced a great save from Ollie Walsh as Keher's extraordinary accuracy saw Kilkenny home. The men in black and amber had won the rubber 4-17 to 6-8, fourteen of those points coming from Keher who was busy becoming the greatest player of his era. Waterford might still have won it but for the brilliant goalkeeping of Ollie Walsh. The greatest era in the county's history had just come to a close.

Tom Cheasty was something of an anomaly. In a team of light and skilful hurlers, he was the odd man out – more of a battering-ram than a rapier. He was from a rural club, Ballyduff, while the team's other stars came from Mount Sion, every inch an urban outfit. But by any standards, Cheasty had an unusual style of play. He crouched over the ball when he carried it in a way that made it almost impossible to dispossess him. For all that, Cheasty was one of the greatest players of his time and without his strength and prowess Waterford would certainly never have made their big breakthrough in the 1950s.

Cheasty made his first mark at inter-county level in the first round of the 1956 Munster Championship, inspiring his team-mates to push a far more experienced Cork team to the wire before losing by six points. From then on, Cheasty was one of the most feared forwards in the game. His style was simple but effective: he loved to get hold of the ball and cut straight down the centre, regardless of how many defenders were in his way. Those glorious runs often ended with him palming the ball over the bar with one of his huge hands. Like Mackey, he was a dramatic player who set the crowd buzzing whenever he gained possession.

There were complaints that Cheasty's striking was unorthodox, but then his inter-county career had been a bit unusual from the start. In 1954 the twenty-year-old Cheasty was in the crowd to watch Waterford play Kilkenny in a National League match. Waterford were so short of players that they resorted to searching the crowd for extra hurlers to make up the numbers. Cheasty, a good club player with Ballyduff, volunteered his services, was drafted in and thus began his stint in the Waterford colours.

Perhaps his style of play can be summed up by one of the most famous scores in his county's history – the point he scored early in the second-half in the drawn 1959 All-Ireland final. With his sights set firmly on the opposition's goal, he took on no less than five strapping Kilkenny defenders, sidestepping a couple of them and shouldering the others out of his way, before striking a perfect shot over the bar. He was completely unstoppable. It was a point no one else could have scored.

Sadly, in 1963 Cheasty became the most high-profile victim of that most blinkered and spiteful of sporting rules, the Ban. That year he had been Man of the Match for Waterford when they won the National League home final against Tipperary. Their reward was a trip to New York to play the home team in the League final proper. From time to time, the GAA hit on the expedient of not crowning the League champions until they had beaten New York, something repeated as recently as 1990 when Kilkenny beat New York by 0-18 to 0-9. Cheasty, however, did not play in New York. He had attended a dance in Waterford organised by a soccer club, was reported and promptly banned from the GAA. If ever an illustration is needed of the petty mentality of the Ban fans, there it is.

Cheasty could have been excused for becoming embittered after this myopic mistreatment. In fact, he rejoined the county team when the Ban was banned and played club hurling well into his forties. In 1996 the Portlaw club held a ceremony in his honour and presented him with the National League medal that was rightly his, even if it was thirty-three years late. It was a happy end to a sorry saga.

THE PERFECTIONISTS

Tipperary, 1960–1965

Munster Champions 1960, 1961, 1962, 1964, 1965

All-Ireland Champions 1961, 1962, 1964, 1965

Like the rest of Ireland, the GAA began to engage in a modernising process in the 1960s. There were a couple of visceral Munster deciders at the start of the decade, but by and large the days of massive flare-ups and pitch invasions were over. RTÉ started broadcasting in 1961, which meant that sport and religion were no longer the sole great communal experiences of the country. People still worried about the outcome of contests between Cork and Tipperary, but quite a few of them also wondered if Dr Richard Kimble would find the one-armed man, or which scandals would unravel in 'Peyton Place'. A groundswell of opinion started to spring up against the Ban, which finally went in 1971. Despite efforts at retrenchment from old-timers and conservatives, it looked as though the GAA would become just another sporting organisation, albeit the one with the greatest hold on the national heartstrings.

You could, of course, entitle this chapter 'The Hard Men', but that would be neither fair nor correct. The Tipperary team of the 1960s remains firmly associated in the public mind with Hell's Kitchen, the appropriately nicknamed full-back line that was probably the most physically fearsome unit ever to play the game. But to focus solely on the physical toughness that underpinned their game is to do the team an injustice – there was far more than brute force and ignorance at work here. For Tipp were the most cerebral of teams. Centre half-back Tony Wall wrote the first in-depth study of hurling, and his team-mates also had a reputation for thinking long and hard about the game.

One skill they had mastered was noting the opposition's weaknesses, which could then be capitalised on in the future. Didn't they even field a player with spectacles – the excellent Matt O'Gara – in two All-Ireland finals? Along with cool intelligence, Tipp were a team with technique and style in spades. With a forward line including Donie Nealon, Sean McLoughlin, Liam Devaney and, the greatest of them all, Jimmy Doyle, flair players one and all, Tipp didn't need to rely on brute force to get their way. Midfielders Theo English and Mick Roche were considerable stylists. When Tipperary really opened up, nobody could live with them.

Yet the idea that they were mainly a physical side has dogged this team's reputation. Cork's Justin McCarthy, who played against them, reckoned that 70% of the team's game consisted of physically intimidating the opposition. This summation, shared by many of McCarthy's contemporaries, overshadows just how good that Tipperary team were. Indeed, had they not hit a complete off-day in the 1963 Munster final, it's likely that Tipp would have won an unprecedented five All-Ireland titles in a row. Had they overcome Waterford that day, it's unlikely that eventual champions Kilkenny would have stood in their way.

Tipperary keeper John O'Donoghue makes the most of the fine protection afforded to him by Hell's Kitchen to field comfortably in the 1965 Munster final. Tipp beat Cork 4-11 to 0-5. As John Doyle said, Tipp did the hurling and Cork did the running.

In 1964 and 1965 nobody, including Kilkenny in a notably one-sided final in 1964, managed to give Tipperary a decent game. The closest anyone came to them in 1964 was fourteen points; in 1965 it was twelve points. Their absolute superiority over all rivals in those golden years has probably never been matched in the history of the hurling championship. Pick any team from the long list of all those who have played and not one of them would have been hopeful of besting the 1964 Tipperary vintage, the team that read as follows:

John O'Donoghue

| John Doyle | Michael Maher | Kieran Carey |

| Mick Burns | Tony Wall | Michael Murphy |

Theo English   Mick Roche

| Jimmy Doyle | Larry Kiely | Babs Keating |

| Donie Nealon | Mackey McKenna | Sean McLoughlin |

THE   START   OF   AN   ERA

But to see how they got to that point, we need to go back to the beginning. Things had been a lot closer for them when the team's run of golden years had gotten underway in 1960, though there were signs of things to come when they scored sixteen goals while defeating Limerick and Waterford in that year's Munster Championship. John Doyle and Jimmy Doyle were in the best form of their career and they needed to be in the 1960 Munster final against Cork, which has been described as the toughest game of hurling ever played.

Cork enjoyed most of the possession in the first-half, but Tipp led by a goal at half-time, largely due to the accuracy of Jimmy Doyle who was to end up with 1-8 to his credit. They stretched their lead to five points in the last quarter, but a last-minute goal from Cork kept the result in doubt right up until the end. The gruelling proceedings ended with Tipperary emerging bloodied but victorious, 4-13 to 4-11, and looking sure to win their first All-Ireland in nine years when they faced Wexford. A certain amount of over-confidence was obvious in the Tipperary camp, most notably in trainer Phil Purcell's comment that no player could mark Jimmy Doyle. It seemed Tipp had tempted fate. In the final, John Nolan did just that, thwarting Doyle at every turn. John Doyle fared no better against Jimmy O'Brien, while Wexford veterans Billy Rackard at centre half-back and Tim Flood at left corner-forward played as well as they'd ever done in Croke Park. Wexford won by 2-15 to 0-11 and Tipperary had learned a valuable lesson.

AN HISTORIC GAME

Tipp set out in pursuit of the Cup again the following year, 1961. That was to be the year that the curtain came down on an era of epoch-making Tipperary Munster final encounters. The two teams faced off in the 1961 final, but with Cork going into decline it would be seven years before the old rivals would meet again in a Munster final that provided any kind of competitive excitement.

Although the 1961 game marked the end of a dozen years of frenzied encounters, it was the biggest of all their clashes – in crowd terms, at least. An official attendance of 62,175 was the biggest ever recorded at a Tipp–Cork match, or indeed at any Irish sporting event outside Croke Park. And the real attendance would, in fact, have been much more, possibly as high as 70,000, because the gates were thrown open halfway through the minor match as the swaying of the densely packed crowd was threatening to lead to panic, or even, ultimately, to a crowd disaster. Thankfully that scenario was averted by the quick action of the stewards.

(The GAA authorities come in for a lot of criticism, some of it deserved, but it is both remarkable and worth remembering that despite all the huge crowds that have attended their games and despite a couple of close shaves, no one has ever died at a GAA match because of crushing or stampeding. There has been no GAA Hillsborough, no Ibrox, no Heysel. The reason for this? A modicum of good luck, certainly, but also the fact that the GAA never failed to throw the gates open when danger threatened, doing themselves out of considerable gate revenue every time. It is one rejoinder to the unfair modern cliché that the GAA puts the making of money above all else.)

The huge crowds in Limerick had an unanticipated and adverse affect on Cork. The Cork players togged out in the Railway Hotel in the town before the game and then travelled in cars to the ground. However, the volume of bodies on the Ennis Road meant that they had to abandon their cars and physically push through the throng to get to the ground. It was no preparation for a big match and by half-time Tipperary were ahead, 3-3 to 0-1, Jimmy Doyle scoring two goals and Donie Nealon the third.

Cork looked to Christy Ring, who had scored 3-4 in the semi-final against Waterford, for one last miracle. Unfortunately, their star was now forty-one years old and reality was about to catch up with the man who had inhabited the world of myth for so long. With Theo English and Liam Devaney in unbeatable form at midfield, Tipperary won by 3-6 to 0-7. Ring's major and most famous contribution on the day was to become embroiled in the second major foul-play controversy of his career. The first had been the Mickey Burke incident eight years previously, this time it was Tom Moloughney of Tipperary who was the victim.

There were eight minutes left when Ring and John Doyle became entangled on the ground. In the resulting fracas, Moloughney was hit with a hurley and had to be taken off, suffering from a wound that necessitated twelve stitches above and below the eye. However, Moloughney never saw the player who had hit him, and RTÉ and the *Irish Independent* were forced to apologise to Ring whom they had reported as the culprit in their match coverage. The fact that the reporters involved were Seán Óg Ó Ceallacháin and the late John D Hickey, paragons of journalistic rectitude both and scarcely controversialists, suggests that the original reports were probably true. Even Val Dorgan, in his biography of Ring, admits he saw Ring hit someone with his hurley. It would have been something of a coincidence if this had been happening at the same time as Moloughney was being struck. On the other hand, Moloughney later said he had seen Ring hit Doyle on the chin with the hurley, so maybe there was, so to speak, a second gunman. The media organisations, however, may have been persuaded to issue apologies by rumours that a different Cork player was prepared to swear, in court and on the Bible, that it was he who had hit Moloughney. It was all pretty murky stuff. Perhaps Moloughney was hit by a hurler on a grassy knoll at the Gaelic Grounds: we await the Oliver Stone movie.

DUBLIN WITHOUT CULCHIES

Tipp's chances of making up for the previous year's All-Ireland slip-up looked much brighter when unfancied Dublin turned over Wexford 7-5 to 4-8 in the Leinster final. This was a new kind of Dublin team, which no longer depended on exiles from strong hurling counties. There was only one culchie on the side, full-forward Paddy Croke from Tipperary. The team was powered by players from the St Vincent's club on the northside of the city, and by the Crumlin club on the southside. So urban was this team it even had a player with an earring, corner-forward Bernard Boothman.

All-Ireland day 1961 and Tipp were hot favourites. This was new territory for the Dubs and in the first-half they looked overawed by the occasion as Tipperary lived up to all the predictions and took a 0-10 to 0-6 lead. The Munster champions looked set to cruise to an easy victory, but a Billy Jackson goal early in the second-half changed everything. The underdogs were in the lead when they suffered a cruel blow: Lar Foley, one of their stars, was sent off, with Tipp's Tom Ryan getting his marching orders in the same incident. Then what looked like a nail in the coffin for Tipp turned out to be a Godsend. The loss of Tony Wall through injury led to Devaney being moved from centre half-forward to centre half-back. In the final quarter, Devaney proceeded to play his best-ever hurling for the county and single-handedly made the difference between victory and defeat.

Dublin might still have won. At the start of the final quarter, with Dublin 1-10 to 0-12 ahead, Billy Jackson fired in a fierce shot, but a great save by Donie O'Brien deflected it over the bar. Nevertheless, Dublin still led by 1-11 to 0-12. Then Tipp, assured under pressure as ever, scored four points in a row – three from Jimmy Doyle frees and one from play by Donie Nealon – to go two clear. A late point by the outstanding Achill Boothman left Tipp just one point ahead, but they held out for a 0-16 to 1-12 victory.

Jimmy Doyle had played a vital role in the game, providing nine of the points, seven of those from frees. His achievement was all the more remarkable considering he had broken his ankle in the Munster final and played on. He hadn't rested the ankle afterwards and was playing in the All-Ireland that day against doctor's orders. The Thurles man received a painkilling injection before the game, another one at half-time, gritted his teeth and played like a demon. His gamble paid off. Donie Nealon must also be mentioned for his haul of three good points from play, which proved vital too. Tipp were back at the top.

SMITH'S WONKY WATCH

In the 1962 campaign, Tipperary nearly came unstuck at the first hurdle when an unrated Limerick team held them to a draw. Referee Jimmy Smith had mistakenly blown for full-time with four minutes left on the clock. Tipperary were leading by a point at the time, but when Smith got the teams back on the field, Limerick managed to level the scores before the real final whistle blew. Tipp, however, made no mistake in the replay, winning 5-13 to 2-4. Their Munster final result against Waterford was remarkably similar, 5-14 to 2-3.

Tipp's nemesis of two years earlier, Wexford, waited in Croke Park to test them again. This was an ageing Wexford team with an incredible six survivors from the 1954 final. Much to the despair of their fans, Wexford got off to possibly the worst start ever by a team in an All-Ireland hurling final. Only one minute of play had elapsed when Tom Moloughney latched onto a Theo English sideline cut and scored a goal. Then the unthinkable happened from the puck-out: the great Nick O'Donnell, who customarily sent the dead ball three-quarterways down the field, mishit the *sliothar*. It fell to Sean McLoughlin just twenty-five yards out and the Tipp corner-forward shot to the net. Wexford were two goals down inside ninety seconds; the crowd in the stadium was dumbfounded.

Remarkably, this did not presage a total collapse by the Wexford oldsters. They drew level near the end of the first-half thanks to a Ned Wheeler goal, although Tipperary re-established control and led by a goal at half-time, 2-6 to 1-6. Early in the second-half a freak Jimmy O'Brien goal reinvigorated Wexford, and with thirteen minutes to go the Leinster champions had actually moved two points clear. But as had happened the year before, Tipp's nerve held better in a tight finish. A Tom Ryan goal put them in front again (this Tom came from Killenaule, his namesake who was sent off the year before came from Toomevara), and though Wexford managed to level with them, late points from Nealon and McLoughlin got Tipp over the line by 3-10 to 2-11.

So Tipperary were back in three-in-a-row territory once again. The 1963 championship campaign began with a comfortable win over Cork, and Waterford,

Tipperary goalkeeper John O'Donoghue and full-back Michael Maher combine to thwart a Cork attack in the 1964 Munster final at the Cork Athletic Grounds.

supine in the previous year's final, were not expected to pose too many problems in the provincial decider. Instead it all went horribly wrong for Tipperary. They were well on top in the first-half, but hit ten wides and at half-time led by only 0-5 to 0-3. Still confidently expecting to pull away in the second-half, they continued to miss chances and gave away frees, which Phil Grimes converted for Waterford to see the outsiders through 0-11 to 0-8. It was one of the shocks of the decade. Tipperary's reaction would tell a great deal about the team's character.

A CASUAL CANTER

In the event, their reaction was superb. For the next two years no team managed to give them a run for their money in the championship. They had twenty points to spare over Clare in the 1964 Munster semi-final, which set up another final clash with Cork. This time, though, there was little for the spectators to get excited about, Tipperary cantered casually in on a scoreline of 3-13 to 1-5, and would have won by far more but for a series of great saves from Cork keeper, Paddy Barry. Tipp would get to spend another day at Croke Park.

John O'Donoghue collects and comes clear against Cork in the 1964 decider, won by 3-13 to 1-5 by a Tipperary team that had no serious rivals at the time.

As reigning All-Ireland champions and staunch local rivals, Kilkenny might have been expected to provide much tougher opposition in that year's All-Ireland final. Indeed, Kilkenny started as marginally higher rated and a very tight game was expected.

So much for expectations. Tipp led by 1-8 to 0-6 at the break, and a real game looked to be in store when John Teehan scored a goal for Kilkenny three minutes into the second-half. But then Tipperary moved up a gear and produced one of the most devastating attacking spells ever launched in an All-Ireland final.

First Jimmy Doyle pointed a free and then Liam Devaney's superb cross-field ball put Nealon in for a goal. The young duo of Babs Keating and Mick Roche added points before Jimmy Doyle set up Sean McLoughlin for a goal. Tipp were 3-12 to 1-7 up and the game was as good as over. By the end, Nealon had scored two more goals to complete his hat-trick and Doyle had amassed ten points. The fourteen-point margin, 5-13 to 2-8, was the biggest All-Ireland final win since Tipp had overwhelmed Laois in the 1949 final.

Jimmy Doyle (wearing Number Ten) watches as the coin is tossed before the start of the 1965 All-Ireland final between Tipperary and Wexford.

If anyone had thought that Tipp's hunger would be dulled by three Cups in four years, then they got their answer in 1965. Their progress to the All-Ireland final in that year was just as imperious, just as majestic. Clare were eviscerated in the Munster semi, and in the provincial final a young Cork team were comprehensively taken apart. Leading 2-4 to 0-4 at half-time, Tipp eventually won by an ego-crushing 4-11 to 0-5. If you had been in the crowd that day and you had voiced the suggestion that Cork would win the following year's All-Ireland and Tipp would get knocked out in the first round of the Munster Championship, the umpires wouldn't have been the only men in white coats bursting into action.

Wexford would be Tipp's opponents in the 1965 final, and anyone expecting a repeat of either the shock of 1960 or the classic of 1962 got short shrift. In the first-quarter, McLoughlin poached two goals in as many minutes, first flicking home a Jimmy Doyle shot and then fielding a Theo English cross and handpassing past keeper Pat Nolan. The destination of the Liam McCarthy Cup was obvious from then on. Tipp led by 2-5 to 0-6 at the break, and 2-16 to 0-10 was the final score. Hell's Kitchen – the firm of Doyle, Maher and Carey – were probably at their most awe-inspiring that day. Tipp's performance was a supreme exhibition of how hurling should be played, although in that form they looked in danger of taking the competitive element out of championship hurling altogether.

TIPP TRIPS

In the end, the Tipp dynasty tumbled in spectacular and surprising style in the 1966 championship. In the first-round game, a young Limerick team looked like providing a routine assignment for the three-in-a-row chasing champions. Tony Wall was serving with the Irish Army in Cyprus, and Jimmy Doyle and Mick Roche were out injured, but that seemed unlikely to make any difference and Tipp went in as favourites. What did make a difference, however, was the display of a twenty-one-year-old Limerick forward named Eamon Cregan who scored 3-5, 3-2 of that from play, as his county caused one of the greatest upsets ever witnessed in hurling. The 4-12 to 2-9 scoreline spelt the end of Tipperary invincibility. Sure they would come back to win Munster titles in 1967 and 1968, losing both All-Ireland finals, but they were nothing like the irresistible force they had been. Hell's Kitchen was broken up – Maher didn't play after 1966, while Carey and Doyle shelved their hurleys after the 1967 campaign. Tony Wall wasn't around in 1968 and neither was Theo English. Tipp, amazingly, were about to go into rapid decline. No sane person would have predicted that either.

Jimmy Doyle was perhaps the greatest stylist among Munster hurling forwards. He didn't achieve the legendary status of Mackey and Ring because he lacked their physical powers: Mackey's strength and Ring's speed were extraordinary and unique, adding a distinct extra dimension to their array of technical skills. With Doyle, however, it was skill all the way. Technically brilliant, he thrived in an age of physical hurling thanks largely to the courage that saw him endure numerous injuries, and often play through them.

If you asked a computer to come up with a blueprint for the ideal hurler, it might produce something like the specifications for Jimmy Doyle. Born in Thurles, he played with the town's famous Sarsfields club for a start. His uncle Tommy had been a key defender on the Tipp three-in-a-row team of the late 1940s and early 1950s, so the sport and the passion ran in his veins. Jimmy enjoyed one of the most impressive under-age careers in the history of the game, scoring 2-8 in the 1955 All-Ireland minor final and 2-3 in the following year's minor decider as Tipperary clocked up a three-in-a-row. He had played in goal in the 1954 final when he was just fourteen years old and his record of appearing in four minor finals in a row has never been and probably never will be beaten.

Small wonder then that this precocious prodigy won his first All-Ireland senior medal in 1958 at the tender age of eighteen, playing left half-forward on the team that beat Galway. He eventually settled down at right half-forward, and in a side full of quality attackers was the undisputed star.

What made Doyle stand out from the crowd was the delicacy of his touch. No matter at what speed or angle the *sliothar* came to him, he was always able to either kill it stone dead or double it with precision. His ability to curve a ball, Brazilian-style, so it duped goalkeepers and defenders, was legendary. And unlike some of the great specialist free-takers he was famously unselfish and keen to lay on scores for his fellow forwards.

Funnily enough, although he ended his career with six All-Ireland medals and a guaranteed place on any 'greatest team of all time' selection, a certain amount of bad luck surrounded Doyle. He was dogged by injury to an extent that other all-time greats were not. In 1968, for example, he came down awkwardly on his heel after scoring a spectacular goal against Wexford in the All-Ireland final and was taken off soon afterwards. In 1970 he had been Man of the Match when Tipperary beat Cork in the Oireachtas Tournament final, but by the following year, when he was just over thirty years old, his career had been so disrupted that he came on only as a sub. in that year's All-Ireland final. He retired soon afterwards. Given how Ring, Mackey and, the greatest of Leinster forwards, Keher did some of their finest hurling well into their thirties, it's no exaggeration to say that a lucky Jimmy Doyle might have challenged for the title of Greatest of Them All. As it is, he's not that far off.

THE RESTORERS

Limerick, 1973–1974

Munster Champions 1973, 1974

All-Ireland Champions 1973

The first half of the 1970s was perhaps the time most comparable to these exuberant Tiger days. Buoyed by the Lemass economic miracle, emigrants began to return home to the small villages of the west and every country town seemed to have a festival with some hybrid between rock group and showband giving it loads in the marquee. Until it all began to fall apart in the middle of the decade, we'd never had it so good.

Even the GAA seemed touched by the new spirit of adventure. There were experiments: the handpass returning in football, the eighty-minute match being adopted in the championship at the end of the 1960s. People at home began to see All-Ireland finals on colour television and team photos usually included a couple of players whose haircuts wouldn't have been out of place on the sleeve of a glam-rock album. Extravagant facial hair had its day in the sun. And teams that had been dormant in the 1960s – Clare, Galway and Limerick – began to make their way back.

When the greatest Limerick team of all time won their third All-Ireland title in 1940, not even the county's greatest pessimist would have predicted that it would be thirty-three years before they would grace the winner's podium again. And when a team trained by Mackey won the 1955 Munster title, few would have reckoned that another eighteen years would elapse before they got their mitts on the provincial crown. To complete our trinity of the unlikely: few would have expected that it would take seven years for the exciting Limerick team that shocked Tipperary in the 1966 Munster Championship to finally land a Munster and All-Ireland title for the county. You'd be inclined to wonder who broke the mirror.

Limerick looked the very definition of likely lads when they proclaimed their arrival with that 1966 win. In fact, it was a surprise when they were edged out in the Munster semi-final that year by Cork. In the end, just two points separated the teams that day, and when the Rebels went on to win that year's All-Ireland it looked certain that Limerick would follow in short order. Then the years passed. And passed. When Limerick, having finally reached a provincial decider in 1971, were beaten by Tipperary, 4-16 to 3-18, it looked unlikely that the promise of 1966 would ever be borne out.

LOADED WITH KNOW-HOW

The year 1973 initially didn't look like it was going to be a particularly vintage year for Limerick. Reaching the National League final was a boost, but losing it to Wexford, 4-13 to 3-7, seemed to confirm that Limerick simply weren't good enough. Still, in the Munster semi-final they revenged the previous year's defeat by Clare, 3-11 to 3-9, to face Tipperary in the final.

An impressive feature of Limerick's progress that year was the willingness of the team's management to countenance drastic positional switches, which just might pay dividends. They had a backroom team loaded with know-how: 1930s legend Jackie Power was coach, while his old team-mate Dick Stokes was chairman of the selectors. Powerful defender Ned Rea had been subjected to heavy criticism for his display at full-back after the League final and his place looked in jeopardy. Instead, he was switched to full-forward where his great physical strength and aerial ability caused havoc for the Tipperary defence. Pat Hartigan was moved to

The Hartigan brothers were not only fine hurlers but also represented Ireland in athletics. Here Pat displays his shot-putting prowess.

full-back while Willie Moore made the move from full-forward line to full-back line.

The 1973 Munster final was an amazing game. Tipperary often seemed primed to break away from the outsiders, finally finishing up with twenty scores to Limerick's thirteen – an unprecedented disparity in such a tight game. The key was Limerick's ability to get goals, including three in the first twenty-four minutes from Frankie Nolan, Richie Bennis and Mossie Dowling. Tipperary still led 2-9 to 3-2 at half-time and stretched their lead to six points early in the second-half. Limerick hung in there and got back into the match with another Nolan goal before Cregan made the decisive move, flashing home two superb goals to leave Limerick 6-3 to 2-13 clear midway through the second-half.

It was tit for tat after that and Limerick moved a point clear with a Richie Bennis-pointed free two minutes from time. Still, Tipp looked like they had survived when John Flanagan, who had scored the winning point in 1971, levelled one minute later.

What happened next, in the dying seconds of the game, was controversial – at least in the eyes of the Tipp followers. A Limerick shot appeared to have gone wide before it struck a Tipperary defender. Nonetheless, a seventy was awarded and Richie Bennis was informed that he would have to make a direct score to win the match as this was the last puck of the game. It was extraordinary pressure to heap on the shoulders of any player, but Bennis was equal to the challenge and struck the *sliothar* over the bar. Even then, some Tipp fans claimed his shot had actually tailed off wide. But jubilant Limerick were unworried by such speculation.

C A R P E   D I E M

After such dramatics, a backlash was inevitable and Limerick were far from impressive when overcoming London – who'd shocked Galway – 1-15 to 0-7 in the All-Ireland semi-final. Limerick would probably have started as rank outsiders against reigning champions Kilkenny in the All-Ireland final had the Leinster champs not suffered an amazing streak of bad luck. Between the Leinster final and the All-Ireland, the Cats lost key players Eamonn Morrissey, who emigrated to Australia, Jim Treacy, to injury, Kieran Purcell, to appendicitis and, worst of all, the great Eddie Keher who broke his collar bone. Limerick saw their chance.

They grabbed that opportunity with both hands and in some style, aided by another brilliant selectorial decision. With Keher and Purcell sidelined, Kilkenny's star attacker would be Pat Delaney, a centre half-forward who was far too quick for most inter-county defenders. So Limerick didn't choose a defender to mark him, instead they switched Eamon Cregan back to the Number Six slot where he played an inspiring game and nullified Delaney.

Above: *All eyes on the prize: the huge concentration and sheer courage exuded by the Clare defence in the 1990s is illustrated by Frank Lohan as he prepares to block a shot by Brian O'Meara of Tipperary.*

Below: *They might have been favourites, but as this picture shows, Limerick were always lagging behind Clare in the historic 1995 Munster final.*

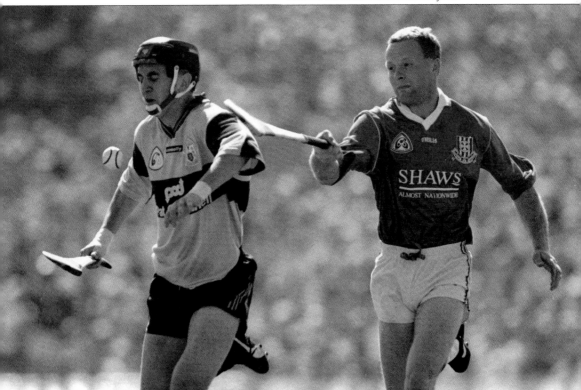

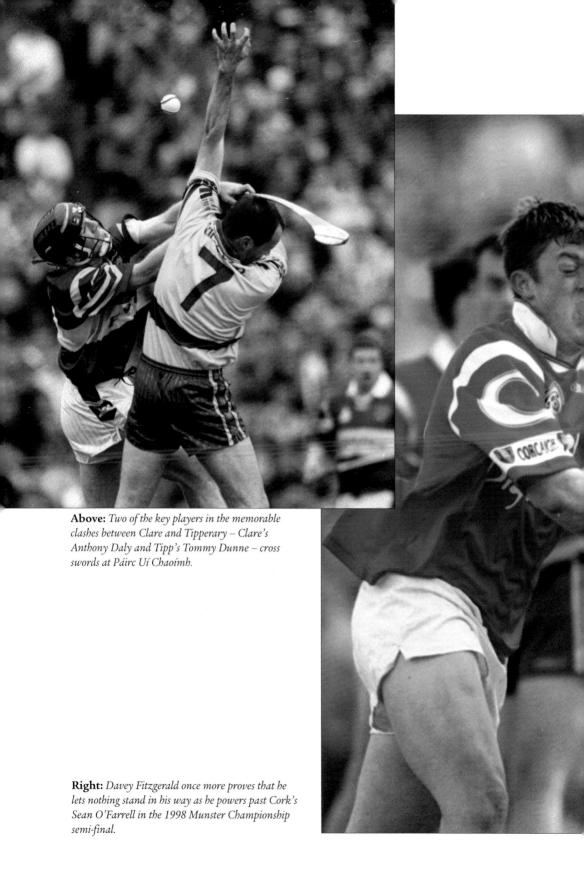

Above: *Two of the key players in the memorable clashes between Clare and Tipperary – Clare's Anthony Daly and Tipp's Tommy Dunne – cross swords at Páirc Uí Chaoímh.*

Right: *Davey Fitzgerald once more proves that he lets nothing stand in his way as he powers past Cork's Sean O'Farrell in the 1998 Munster Championship semi-final.*

Above: *Clare's best attacker, Jamesie O'Connor, seen here galloping away from Clem Smith of Limerick.*

Below: *Ferocious goalmouth exchanges in the 1997 All-Ireland final as Brian Lohan and Michael O'Halloran of Clare try to deny Liam Cahill of Tipperary.*

Above: *Liam Doyle, the epitome of an unsung hero and one of the finest wing-backs of his generation, manages to clear past a determined Eddie Tucker of Tipperary.*

Below: *The Moment of Truth. Despite the attentions of Brian Lohan in the 1997 All-Ireland final between Tipperary and Clare, Eugene O'Neill (Number Fourteen) doubles on the ball and finds the net to put Tipp a goal up with three minutes left. Clare scored their most dramatic victory of all thanks to late points from Ollie Baker and Jamesie O'Connor.*

Opposite: *The great Sean McMahon in typically dominant form as he rises above Tipperary's Declan Ryan.*

Above: *Half a hurley might be better than none, but five percent of one is no use to any man: Ollie Baker finds himself playing with a cocktail stick after this clash with Tipperary's Aidan Butler. Jamesie O'Connor watches the fallout.*

Above: *Things start to get seriously nutty in The Match That Launched A Thousand Phone Calls. Michael White clatters Brian Lohan with his* camán *as all the bad feeling underlying the 1998 Munster final replay between Waterford and Clare begins to get an airing.*

Below: *Brian Lohan lands a straight left on Michael White, ensuring his sending-off and suspension.*

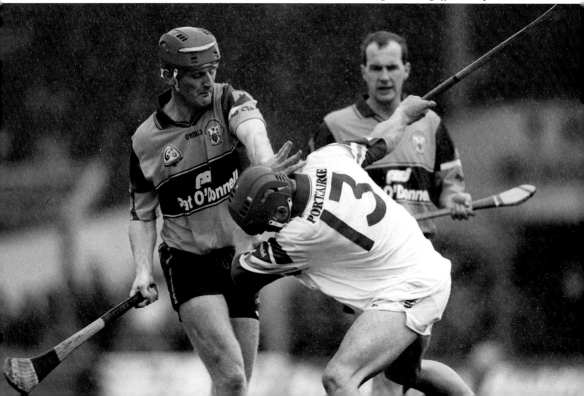

On a wet day, Limerick led by two points at half-time, 0-12 to 1-7, with Pat Delaney bagging the Kilkenny goal. Kilkenny drew level within six minutes of the restart with points from Claus Dunne and Chunky O'Brien. Then the game turned on two incidents: Limerick keeper Seamus Horgan made a magnificent save from Mick Crotty and shortly afterwards a poor puck-out by Horgan's opposite number, Noel Skehan, gave Mossie Dowling the chance to scramble in a goal that looked like the hurling equivalent of rugby's pushover try. But the quality didn't matter to Limerick, they had waited long enough. They were All-Ireland champions on a 1-21 to 1-14 scoreline.

DROUGHT ... RAIN ... DROUGHT

After such a dramatic breakthrough, it was probably difficult for Limerick to recapture the same intensity the following year, but they still made it two Munster titles in a row with a 6-14 to 3-9 win over Clare. In the All-Ireland final Kilkenny had their

Limerick get off to a dream start in the 1973 Munster final as Frankie Nolan (left) scores an early goal against Tipperary in Thurles.

revenge, winning 3-19 to 1-13, and this Limerick team faded away after that. But they had made a valuable contribution to their county's hurling history. Incredible as it may seem, but for that lone victory it would now be sixty-two years since the county had won an All-Ireland title. As it stands, it's only eighteen years – and counting.

The Limerick 1973 vintage was a good one and would probably have won more All-Ireland titles had they not been playing at a particularly competitive time. Pat Hartigan, an international shot-putter, was the finest full-back of the era. Pat's brother, right half-forward Bernie, was a hammer-thrower of genuine class who once, on the same day, won a European Cup fixture for Ireland and destroyed thousands of pounds worth of electronic recording equipment with a stray hammer throw. Old kingpins Ahane had no representatives on this team, which had a major input from two clubs in particular: sharpshooter extraordinaire Richie Bennis, his brother Phil, stylish wing-back Sean Foley and opportunist corner-forward Frankie Nolan all hailed from Patrickswell; Pat Hartigan, Eamonn Grimes, 1973 Hurler of the Year, and corner-forward Joe McKenna played for South Liberties. And, above all and beyond all, there was Eamon Cregan from Claughaun.

The Limerick team that bridged a gap of thirty-three years by defeating Kilkenny in the All-Ireland final of 1973.

Seamus Horgan

Willie Moore   **Pat Hartigan**   **Jim O'Brien**

Phil Bennis   **Eamon Cregan**   **Sean Foley**

Richie Bennis   **Eamonn Grimes**

Bernie Hartigan   **Mossie Dowling**   **Liam O'Donoghue**

Frankie Nolan   **Ned Rea**   **Joe McKenna**

Few people ever doubted that Eamon Cregan would be a major inter-county star. Hadn't he scored two great goals in the 1965 Munster semi-final to give Limerick a shock win over Cork? Actually, that was a football game, and there are those who say that had Cregan been born in a football county he would have been one of the best at that sport, too. That sums up the kind of career Cregan enjoyed. He exuded confidence in his own ability and was the sort of disciplined and efficient player you could trust to do anything he put his mind to.

Who also would have had the guts to switch from corner-forward to centre half-back for the 1973 All-Ireland final and still look a class apart in the new position against one of the great attackers of the modern game, Pat Delaney? And when Limerick were on the verge of being completely overwhelmed in the 1980 All-Ireland final by a rampant Galway side, Cregan fought an almost single-handed battle to turn the tide, which almost succeeded. He scored 2-7 that day, including a memorable overhead goal and a point where he showed Conor Hayes the ball and then nonchalantly drove a shot over the bar from out on the left sideline. 'Look,' he seems to be saying, 'this is what I'm going to do and there's no way you're going to stop me.'

Cregan always seemed to have a professional attitude, to be a new-model hurler – fit, tactically astute and articulate. The fact that he now manages a golf course in Newcastle West underlines this: it's not a job you could easily imagine Mick Mackey, Christy Ring, or John Doyle doing.

Off the field, Cregan has always been just as much a force to be reckoned with. Quickly gaining a name as one of the best coaches in the business, he led Offaly to victory in the 1994 All-Ireland final; the irony was that Limerick were the Faithful County's victims. He also had the bad luck to be ballyragged by a furious Ger Loughnane after Clare's All-Ireland win over Tipperary in 1997. Cregan's perfectly reasonable post-match analysis that the game wouldn't be remembered as a classic because there had been quite a few mistakes got Loughnane's goat, probably because it didn't take into account how passionate Clare felt about the game. But emoting was never Cregan's thing, his style of play and his personality was a triumph of clinical control over emotional reaction.

But that isn't to say that the man lacked passion. Before the 1973 All-Ireland final, he is reputed to have got himself locked in one of the dressing-room toilets in Croke Park. Undeterred, Cregan charged down the door and hit the pitch running. Like I said, he gave the impression he could do anything.

THE ARISTOCRATS

Cork, 1975–1979

Munster Champions 1975, 1976, 1977, 1978, 1979

All-Ireland Champions 1976, 1977, 1978

Cork hurlers are confident. Their enemies would say they border on arrogant; admirers of the game as played in the county would say that the aristocratic mien of a Cork side in full flight is something special. Like their neighbours, the Kerry footballers, at their best Cork's hurling men brook no opposition. And so it was with their three-in-a-row team of the 1970s. Pushed almost to breaking-point on a number of occasions by Clare, most notably, in Munster and by Wexford beyond the border, they nevertheless gave the impression at all times of being sure of their superiority. That Cork team were the ultimate proof of the old definition of class as grace under pressure.

What is often glossed over is that their magnificent three-in-a-row was bookended by two shock defeats against a resurgent Galway. The 1975 Munster semi-final loss raised real doubts about the quality of the Cork team, while the 1979 defeat signalled the end of an era. In between, however, they were unbeatable, pulling off the first three-in-a-row since an earlier bunch of Rebels had worked the trick in 1954. No one has come near emulating them since. And, interestingly enough, in each of those three consecutive winning years, Christy Ring, at that time a selector, made a memorable intervention.

Even in retirement, Ring worked his magic for his county. Cork's unshakeable confidence was well-founded. Their attack alone contained Ray Cummins, chosen on the GAA millennium team as the finest full-forward of all time, Seanie O'Leary, the doyen of goal-scorers, Jimmy Barry-Murphy, one of the most naturally gifted players ever, and Charlie McCarthy, a showman who lost little caste when compared to the other three. There was the trio of prodigious youngsters – Dermot McCurtain, Johnny Crowley and

Tom Cashman – and a superb supporting cast who often snatched the headlines from the stars. Pat Moylan, for example, was Man of the Match in the 1976 All-Ireland final, Tim Crowley in the decider two years later, and John Horgan was named Hurler of the Year in 1978. For their opponents, weaknesses were extremely hard to find.

Cork were backboned by an extraordinary flowering at club level, which produced three of the finest club teams in the history of the game: Blackrock, Glen Rovers and St Finbarr's. Between 1972 and 1979, Cork clubs won every single All-Ireland club title – except for the 1976 final when Blackrock lost to Kilkenny's James Stephens – Blackrock bagging three, and Glen Rovers and St Finbarr's two each. In fact, winning the Cork title was far more difficult than beating the best teams from the rest of the country. As a result, those players who excelled on the Cork circuit proved to be some of the most talented hurlers of all time. The Rockies had John Horgan, Pat Moylan, Ray Cummins, Brendan Cummins, Dermot McCurtain, Tom Cashman and Kilkenny star Frank Cummins. The Glen lined out with Martin Doherty, Denis Coughlan and Pat Horgan. The 'Barrs could call on Gerald McCarthy, Charlie McCarthy, Jimmy Barry-Murphy and Con Roche. There will probably never be a county championship of that calibre again.

THE MEASURE OF SUCCESS

Under-age titles generally provided a good yardstick for measuring the future strength of a county: Cork won three minor titles in a row between 1969 and 1971 and four under-21 titles on the trot between 1968 and 1971. The 1971 under-21 team, by the way, scored the frankly frightening total of thirty goals in five games. Eight of the players from that team went on to win senior medals later in the decade. There was definitely something special brewing in the south, so it was no surprise when Cork won the 1975 Munster title after easy wins over Waterford, Clare and Limerick. In those three games they had scored twelve goals while only conceding one themselves. Everyone eagerly awaited their All-Ireland final clash with a strong and capable Kilkenny team.

But they had to go on waiting because Galway, who had fallen away to a shocking extent since the 1950s, suddenly decided that they were fed up being the sick men of hurling. In an incredible semi-final they hit three goals within the first ten minutes and held on bravely in the second-half against a fierce Cork backlash. Galway won by 4-15 to 2-19 and they haven't returned to their job as whipping boys since. The entire county of Cork was in shock, and when Kilkenny hammered the Tribesmen in the final, the Rebels had to accept that they were even further off the pace than they had thought. It was a grim day for Cork hurling.

Though they would hate to countenance the idea, Tipperary probably did their deadliest rivals a great favour in 1976 by giving them the kind of tough game they hadn't been subjected to the previous year. Tipp roared into an early lead, firmly throwing down the gauntlet at Cork's feet. Undaunted, Jimmy Barry-Murphy got Cork back in the game and they played some of their finest hurling. Seanie O'Leary scored the winning point in a 4-10 to 2-15 victory. But the Rebels had rode their luck at times: a long free by John Fenton that was fumbled into the net by keeper Seamus Shinnors, and a late shot by a Tipp forward that came back off the post perhaps indicated that this was going to be Cork's year, promising the exact mix of skill and luck needed to get through.

Eamon Cregan did his best to upset that prognosis in the Munster final, but despite his remarkable contribution of four goals and a point, Cork still defeated Limerick easily enough, 3-15 to 4-5. In the All-Ireland final Wexford took centre stage, having ended Kilkenny's three-in-a-row dreams with a remarkable seventeen-point victory in the Leinster final. The meeting of Wexford and Cork was bound to evoke memories of the 1950s finals and early signs suggested that this was going to be a repeat of 1956 rather than 1954 – when Martin Quigley scored two goals and the Slaneysiders led 2-2 to no score after six minutes.

The Cummins sandwich: brothers Ray (right) *and Brendan close in on Wexford full-back Willie Murphy in the 1976 All-Ireland final.*

The unstoppable Ray Cummins heads for goal in the 1976 All-Ireland final.

OLD SCORES SETTLED

But this was 1976 and Pat Moylan was having the game of his life. The Blackrock midfielder scored a series of inspirational long-range points and the inevitable Ray Cummins goal left the teams level at the break, Cork 1-11, Wexford 2-8. Tony Doran gave Wexford the perfect start to the half with a first-minute goal, but two minutes later Charlie McCarthy replied with the goal of the game as he met a long Brendan Cummins ball with a spectacular half-volley. In the second-half the game developed into what was arguably the finest final of that decade.

With Mick Jacob outstanding at centre half-back and Mick Butler scoring the Slaneysiders fourth goal, the Leinster champs led by two points with only eight minutes left. With the two sides so evenly matched in terms of strength, skill and speed, it was tactical *nous* that proved to be the difference in the end.

Ten minutes from time, Cork switched Jimmy Barry-Murphy to centre half-forward. Enjoying the extra space and benefitting from Jacob's fatigue after playing so well for so long, Barry-Murphy fired over three match-winning points and Moylan, fittingly, had the final score. Cork had squeezed through by 2-21 to 4-11. On the platform afterwards, Christy Ring made a speech, remarkable for its generosity and prescience,

Close-quarter exchanges in the 1976 Munster final between Cork and Limerick.

declaring: 'My hurling days are over, but let no one say that the best hurlers belong to the past. They are with us now and better yet to come.' Other former greats spent their time bemoaning an imagined decline in the standard of hurling, but Ring was never a man to follow the pack.

A NEW PRETENDER

In 1977 Cork had a new threat to contend with. Clare, who had been also-rans in Munster since 1932, seemed to have finally come up with a team to challenge the best.

Their half-back line of Ger Loughnane, Sean Hehir and Sean Stack was probably the best in the game. They showed they meant business by annexing the National League title with a persuasive win over Kilkenny. Their manager was the apostle of rural development, Fr Harry Bohan, but they were coached by Justin McCarthy – a fact that was to prove a bone of contention.

McCarthy, from the Cork City suburb of Rochestown, had won an All-Ireland medal with Cork in 1966 before a potentially brilliant career was hampered and eventually cut short by injuries received in a motorbike accident. McCarthy stayed in the game and went on to coach Cork in 1975. They were defeated in the semi-final that year, and McCarthy suffered a barrage of criticism. Many people felt, and still feel, that he was used as a scapegoat. In October 1976, Fr Bohan asked McCarthy to take over as Clare coach. He accepted and moved to the Banner county.

The trinity of St Finbarr's, Glen Rovers and Blackrock made the Cork county championships of the 1970s unforgettable, and between them they took seven out of eight All-Ireland titles. Here, St Finbarr's Christy Ryan clashes with Teddy O'Brien and Martin Doherty of Glen Rovers in the 1977 senior county final. The 'Barrs won and went on to succeed the Glen as All-Ireland champions.

A perfectionist and a fiercely independent character in an organisation run by men who regarded conformity as one of the cardinal virtues, McCarthy's work with Clare made him something of a hate figure for certain elements within the Cork County Board. His presence added a real edge to the Cork–Clare rivalry of the time.

LET THE GAMES BEGIN

Round one between the teams was the 1977 Munster final. At one stage it looked as though Cork wouldn't even make it that far as they trailed Waterford by eight points just ten minutes into the second-half of their semi-final match. It required all of Cork's brilliance to get out of that particular fix before coming through by 4-13 to 3-11.

Perhaps the biggest winners of all on Munster final day in Thurles was the team of armed robbers who got away with £24,579 in gate receipts during the second-half. It was a nasty and costly reminder that Ireland was becoming a very different place from the type of country represented by the GAA. Meanwhile, back on the field, Clare got off to a criminally bad start when they conceded a penalty after seventy-five seconds. Tim Crowley duly sent it to the net. Instead of crumbling, they responded magnificently, full-forward Noel Casey skinning Martin Doherty to first set up a goal for Enda O'Connor and then score a goal himself. Clare were 2-4 to 1-1 up and Cork looked in danger of being swept aside.

Once more, though, the Corkmen kept the head and calmly appraised the situation, exploiting the advantage Jimmy Barry-Murphy had over his marker, Gus Lohan. By the twentieth minute Barry-Murphy had scored one goal and set up Charlie McCarthy for another to put Cork ahead. The game was still very much up for grabs coming up to half-time when one of those incidents which always seem to dog the bridesmaid counties finished Clare off. Full-back Jim Power, who had been involved in a physical battle with Ray Cummins from the get-go, finally lost his temper in spectacular style and struck the Cork full-forward. The Banner were just a point down at half-time, but everyone knew their chance had gone with Power's dismissal. They battled hard in the second-half and weren't disgraced by losing 4-15 to 4-10.

Galway lined up once more in the All-Ireland semi-final, but there was to be no repeat of the 1975 shock. Cork got out of the traps quickly this time with a couple of early goals, endured a few rocky moments in the third-quarter and finally put the Connacht side away with a Seanie O'Leary goal that ensured a resounding 3-14 to 1-15 victory.

Their final opposition would be Wexford, who had scotched any notion that their win over Kilkenny the previous year had been a freak result by beating the Cats 3-17 to 3-14 in the Leinster final, which was a more comprehensive victory than the scoreline suggests. Their towering full-forward Tony Doran – the Nicky Rackard of his day – was in superb form, and the Leinster champions really fancied their chances of taking revenge. Another classic looked to be in store.

DOHERTY DESTROYS DORAN

Sadly, wet and windy weather conditions on All-Ireland day affected both teams and Wexford, in particular, never really got going. Martin Doherty had one of his finest games for Cork as he blotted out Doran for most of the match. The veteran Denis Coughlan gave an exhibition at left half-back, and Gerald McCarthy's dominance at centre half-forward gave the rest of the Cork attack the platform to strike the

The old master and the young pretender: Christy Ring passes on some words of advice to Jimmy Barry-Murphy at Páirc Uí Chaoímh as Cork prepare for the 1978 Munster final against Clare.

match-winning scores. McCarthy's move to the Number Eleven berth had been proposed by Ring, and it worked wonderfully. But the man of the day was undoubtedly Seanie O'Leary, the Youghal corner-forward whose eye for goal has never been equalled in the modern era. During the warm-up, O'Leary's nose was broken when he received a belt of the *sliothar*, but he opted to play on and turned out to be the controversial matchwinner.

The controversy arose from a change in policy. The GAA had brought in a rule stipulating that players could not drop the hurley deliberately in order to make it easier for them to handpass the ball to the net. That seemed to be exactly what O'Leary did when scoring Cork's only goal in the second-half, but the goal was allowed to stand. At the time it didn't look as though it mattered because Wexford looked dead and buried anyway. However, Doran finally began to get some change from Doherty, and Wexford launched a desperate and impressive late rally. Two goals brought them back into the match, and they would have earned a scarcely deserved replay but for Martin Coleman. The Ballinhassig man is constantly underrated, but he got Cork out of trouble yet again with a splendid diving save to push away a Christy Kehoe shot that was sneaking in at the post three minutes from the end. (The GAA's tendency towards dynastic narrative

Above: *Charlie McCarthy* (right) *and Tim Crowley* (left), *two of Cork's key attackers in the 1970s, close in on Noel O'Dwyer of Tipperary.*

Opposite: *One of the finest wing-backs of the 1970s, Dermot McCurtain clears for Cork in the 1978 Munster final against Clare, a day when the Rebels were saved by their defence.*

was underlined when Coleman's son, also named Martin, played in goal for the Cork minor team that won last year's All-Ireland final.)

Cork beat Wexford 1-17 to 3-8 and the three-in-a-row was very much on. As had been the case so often before, it looked as though their toughest task would be getting out of Munster because this looked to be the year Clare were finally going to overcome their ghosts. The Banner had been simply sensational when defeating Kilkenny 3-14 to 0-12 in the National League final, and their Munster semi win over Limerick, 4-12 to 3-8, added to the conviction that this was going to be Clare's year.

The biggest Munster final crowd since 1961 – 54,181 bodies to be exact – was there in Thurles to see Clare's attempt to dethrone Cork. A sizeable proportion of people there

Two modern greats: Jimmy Barry-Murphy gets in a shot in the 1978 All-Ireland final while Kilkenny's Joe Hennessy looks on. The Kilkenny banner, 'A little Hennessy beats your Murphys', didn't prove to be true on the day.

that day must have thought they were about to see history being made. Such was the volume of people in and around the stadium that, in scenes reminiscent of the 1961 final, John Horgan, Cork's left corner-back, got stuck in traffic and would have missed the match had he not been able to persuade some gardaí to escort him to the ground. Those lawmen could not have known that their decent gesture would prove to have a profound effect on the events of the day.

'IT'S NOW OR NEVER'

By half-time it looked as though Clare were about to make the breakthrough, primarily because, for the first and only time, the Cork attack was a shambles. Cork's forwards had failed to score at all in the first-half, shooting thirteen wides, and their 0-5 to 0-3 half-time lead was due to three points garnered by the tardy Horgan from long-distance frees, another from a seventy and one point coming from midfielder Tom Cashman, Cork's other outstanding performer on the day. However, that hair's breadth two-point lead didn't look at all sufficient in the face of Clare's determination. The jubilant fans gave Clare an ovation as they went off at half-time.

Then there was divine intervention – in the form of Christy Ring. At the break he lifted the Corkmen with a rousing speech that included the unforgettable lines: 'When I played against Clare, I could beat them on my own. There are *fifteen* of ye.' Clare, on the other hand, seemed to freeze just when the finishing line was in sight. That week's *Clare Champion* had run the headline: 'It's now or never'. As the second-half wore on, Clare seemed unable to make it now and gradually became resigned to it being never. With ten minutes left Cork were 0-12 to 0-7 ahead, and even a late rally from Clare couldn't get them any closer than 0-13 to 0-11. Their last-gasp chance came when a shot from Ger Loughnane dropped just over the bar. At the final whistle, a distraught Loughnane dropped to his knees and beat the ground with his fists. Clare, we thought, were destined for perpetual failure; Loughnane, it turned out, did not agree.

The Munster final had been such a tense, nail-biting affair that the All-Ireland final proved to be a bit of an anti-climax. The old enemy, Kilkenny, were the opposition and they gave Cork a fright when Kevin Fennelly struck for an early goal after a defensive mix-up. The Rebels, however, looked stronger overall in most areas of the field and came through by 1-15 to 2-8, the deadly Barry-Murphy sealing victory with a typical opportunist goal. Charlie McCarthy weighed in with seven points, while Horgan ensured Hurler of the Year status with another classic display. But the man of the match was the often unsung Tim Crowley. The burly Newcestown man took over at midfield when switched there from left half-forward and swung over one memorable point from the sideline, which seemed to highlight the difference in skill between the two sides.

When Cork won their fifth Munster title in a row the following year, by defeating Limerick 2-14 to 0-9, the Holy Grail of four All-Irelands in a row looked a distinct possibility. But this team's story ended as it had started: with a Galway ambush. The semi-final should, in theory, have been a walkover, but Galway confounded expectation yet again. Goals by Finbarr Gantley and Noel Lane gave the westerners a 2-14 to 1-13 win, thereby confirming that a new power was abroad in the land. It might have been an ignoble way to finish, but it's some small comfort that the equal of that 1970s Cork side hasn't been seen since.

Ray Cummins takes on the Limerick defence in the 1979 Munster final. Cork won 2-14 to 0-9, but Galway were waiting in the long grass.

Martin Coleman

Brian Murphy   Martin O'Doherty   John Horgan

Dermot McCurtain   John Crowley   Denis Coughlan

Tom Cashman   Pat Moylan

Jimmy Barry-Murphy   Gerald McCarthy   Tim Crowley

Charlie McCarthy   Ray Cummins   Seanie O'Leary

(Subs John Allen, Eamonn O'Donoghue)

When you watched Ray Cummins playing full-forward, the phrase that sometimes came to mind was, 'It's not fair.' After all, the man was well over six-feet tall, had perhaps the best catching hand in hurling and was so strong he couldn't be knocked off the ball once he had it in his possession. At his best, there was an air of inevitability about Cummins. When the *sliothar* was in the Cork full-forward's hand and he turned towards goal, it was time for the umpire to dust down the green flag.

It says everything about Cummins's talent that he stood out as the best full-forward in the game during a heroic age of Number Fourteens. Tony Doran of Wexford and Joe McKenna of Limerick were doing the rounds at the same time, and they too were big men who could take any amount of punishment and were unstoppable if on song. In comparison with the present era when goal-scoring seems to have largely gone out of fashion, the regularity with which those men found the net looks even more remarkable. For all that, Cummins was unarguably the best of the lot.

Strangely, the big Blackrock man won his first major honour as a left half-back, appearing there for the Cork team that won the 1968 All-Ireland title. By the following year he was occupying full-forward on the senior side that lost the All-Ireland final against Kilkenny.

Kilkenny got the better of Cummins, and Cork, again in 1972, but he did give one of the finest ever All-Ireland displays by a losing hurler, scoring 2-3 from play. In the 1976 final he scored a vital 1-2 against Wexford. But what was equally important throughout his career was the host of scores he created and set up for his team-mates. Full-backs gladly gave away frees to halt Cummins while he unselfishly laid off a lot of the ball he won. At his peak, he was simply unplayable.

Like his partner-in-crime, Jimmy Barry-Murphy, Cummins was also a superb footballer, winning an All-Ireland medal with Cork in 1973. If that legendary Kerry team had not appeared in the mid-1970s, Cork might well have achieved the unprecedented feat of completely dominating football and hurling at the same time.

And then, of course, there was the 1982 Munster final – the final Waterford people still shudder to think of. Cork were nearly thirty points ahead of the Waterfordians when Cummins got through on goal. He could have buried the ball in the back of the net, but instead he handpassed it over the bar. It was a sporting gesture. It took a big man to make it.

THE REVIVALISTS

Tipperary, 1987–1993

Munster Champions 1987, 1988, 1989, 1991, 1993

All-Ireland Champions 1989, 1991

Now that they're back, it's hard to credit the slump Tipperary hurling fell into between the early 1970s to mid-1980s. Strong counties had suffered poor runs before – Cork went without an All-Ireland title between 1954 and 1966, and Kilkenny didn't win one between 1947 and 1957 – but no one suffered a famine of this magnitude. The stark fact is that between 1971 and 1987, Tipp didn't win a single Munster title. An even worse narrative of decrepitude hides behind that statistic. It wasn't as if Tipperary were narrowly missing out on provincial honours, or were in there competing with the big boys but just not getting the breaks. The only finals they made in their wilderness years were those of 1973, 1984 and 1985. A lot of the time they weren't at the races at all. Between 1974 and 1983, Tipp didn't win a single match in the Munster Championship.

Tipp's malaise was symptomatic of a time when Munster was no longer the dominant force. In the 1980s, for example, the province amassed just three All-Ireland titles, Munster's worst-ever showing in a decade. This was due to the arrival of two major new forces. Galway finally delivered on their promise and won titles in 1980, 1987 and 1988, and the neophytes of Offaly won the 1981 and 1985 finals. Tipperary, and to a lesser extent Cork, learned that they had no divine right to win, that tradition would be of little help against teams determined to overturn the old order. After the Cork three-in-a-row team departed the scene, no outstanding side emerged in the province until Tipp's late 1980s resurrection.

They might have fallen on hard times, but they never lost their confidence. A border guard patrols the frontier between Tipperary and Kilkenny.

He might not be everyone's cup of tea (the Offaly players obviously couldn't put up with him when he was in charge there, for a start), but Michael 'Babs' Keating's role in Tipperary's return to the big time should not be played down. He took over an unfancied Tipp team and proved to be an inspiring leader, with former team-mates Theo English and Donie Nealon as his dependable sidekicks.

Keating had been a young member of the great 1960s Tipp team and went on to play a key role in the 1971 All-Ireland win when he was arguably the best forward in the country. Loud, opinionated, astute and with boundless belief in his own ability, he was an ideal manager for a county struggling to regain their confidence. Babs was flash – his idea of raffling a racehorse to raise money for the team's training fund was evidence of that. Upon taking over, he also pioneered the Supporters' Clubs, which have proved such a vital fund-raising tool for counties ever since. Babs also spoke his mind: the old GAA tradition of being careful not to give offence and hiding behind false modesty held no appeal for him.

JEWELS IN THE CROWN

Even the best manager needs special players to win an All-Ireland, and Pat Fox and Nicky English were the jewels in Keating's crown. From the outside, they were diametrical opposites. Fox was stocky and gave the impression of having to work hard at his game. He had begun as a corner-back and perpetually struggled with a serious knee-ligament injury, which had almost ended his career. English, on the other hand, looked naturally gifted and elegant in everything he did. He was an instinctive forward

Aerial Warfare: the extraordinary athleticism of top hurlers was rarely better caught than in this shot of Cork's Teddy McCarthy soaring high to win the ball in the drawn 1987 Munster final against Tipperary.

who had won All Stars back in 1983, 1984 and 1985 when Tipp were still in the doldrums. Fox appeared animated by a ferocious hunger; English was sometimes accused of being too laid-back. But they were the outstanding corner-forwards of their day, a pair of irresistible scoring machines when the mood took them.

It was the forwards who made this Tipp team. The backs were competent enough, but could concede big scores. Often it didn't matter because the forwards would cancel those out at the other end. By 1989 English and Fox had been joined up front by the brilliant young duo of John Leahy and Declan Ryan, the uncannily accurate Michael Cleary, and the Viking-lookalike, battering-ram full-forward Cormac Bonnar. There hadn't been a better attacking sextet in decades. Indeed, Tipperary played so much good hurling in their years at the top that they were reminiscent of the great Limerick side of the 1930s. Despite their successes, they still gave the impression of having slightly underachieved, of having just missed out on an extra few All-Irelands.

The Babs revival got off to a stumbling start when Tipp nearly came a cropper against Clare in the Munster semi-final in 1987. They were held to a draw by a late Gerry McInerney goal, but completely overpowered Clare in the replay, winning 4-17 to 0-8, with 3-11 coming from Fox and English. The convincing winning margin made people sit up and take notice. Still, they would start the Munster final as outsiders against a powerful Cork side whose semi-final win over Limerick had included the John Fenton goal widely regarded as the greatest of all time – a first-time shot that flew straight into the net from forty yards out.

Cork were reigning All-Ireland champions and had ruthlessly put paid to promised Tipperary revivals in 1984 and 1985. But this game would take place in Semple Stadium in front of fanatical home supporters who dared to believe that they'd witness something special. They were right. Tipperary led by 0-11 to 0-7 at the break, and a brilliant goal by English put them seven points clear early in the second-half. Hurley knocked out of his hand as he was going through, the Lattin-Cullen man kept his cool, controlled the ball with his foot and calmly sidefooted it past Ger Cunningham. It looked like a match-winning piece of improvisation, but yet again Tipp stalled with the chequered flag in view. A string of points brought Cork back into the game, and three minutes from time they moved two points ahead when Kieran Kingston scored a goal. Somehow, Tipp rallied and two pointed frees from Fox earned them a draw and another chance.

'YE HAVEN'T HURLED AT ALL'

Killarney was the venue for the replay. The first-half seemed to confirm the general opinion that Tipperary had blown their big chance in Thurles. Cork rattled off five points without reply in the first ten minutes and led 1-10 to 1-5 by half-time, a superb

English goal being cancelled out by a Tomas Mulcahy effort. Playing well and with the wind in their favour in the second-half, Cork looked home and dry. During the break in the Tipp dressing room, an impassioned Donie Nealon told the players that the game was there to be won, 'Ye haven't hurled at all and it's still there waiting for ye.'

An inspired Tipperary played their best half of hurling for many years and dragged themselves back into contention with a succession of points. They even got over the disaster of seeing a Pat Fox goal ruled out because the umpires thought the shot had come off the post rather than the stanchion supporting the net. Twelve minutes from time a great Fox point finally brought the two teams level. Nerves would be severely wracked from here on in. Cork regained the lead twice and Tipp levelled twice before a Fenton free left the Rebels a point clear with time fast running out. Then, right at the death, English tore through the Cork defence and handpassed over the bar for a fantastic solo equaliser. Extra time would settle this thing once and for all.

The famine is over: a battered and deliriously happy Richard Stakelum is chaired from the field in Killarney after Tipperary's 4-22 to 1-12 win had given them their first Munster title in sixteen years.

In extra time an unlikely but oddly fitting hero emerged. Michael Doyle had never had an easy job making his way as an inter-county hurler. As son of the legendary John, he was always destined to be compared unfavourably to his old man. Perhaps that is why the sons of the immortals never match the deeds of their fathers. Certainly, the younger Doyle seemed doomed to be remembered forever as the man who had lost the *sliothar* in the 1984 final, which led directly to Cork's winning score. Now, brought on at full-forward, he would finally exorcise that centenary spectre.

Cork led 1-21 to 1-20 after the first period of extra time, but Tipp moved into the lead with points from Fox and Donie O'Connell. And when Doyle found the net after an O'Connell shot had been blocked, the tide turned comprehensively their way. Doyle took a pass from Pat Fitzelle, rampaged through and handpassed past Ger Cunningham for his second goal. An O'Connell goal created by Fox gave Tipp an incredible 4-22 to 1-22 victory.

Captain and right half-back Richard Stakelum gave one of the most memorable of all Munster final victory speeches, roaring defiantly, 'the famine is over', before leading the crowd in a rendition of 'Slievenamon'. Babs and his boys had done the trick. It had been a remarkable feat of clever management: eleven changes had been made to the team that had been knocked out by Clare in 1986.

TACKLING THE TRIBESMEN

Tipp had reached such emotional heights in getting back to the top in Munster that it was probably a bit much to expect them to go on and take the All-Ireland. They played their part well in a superb All-Ireland semi-final against Galway, but the greater experience of the westerners – who had been beaten finalists in 1985 and 1986 – told in the end. But it was a close-run thing at times. Galway blitzed Tipp early on and were 1-4 to 0-1 up after seven minutes, thanks to a terrific goal by wing-forward Martin Naughton. Tipp clawed their way back into the game and by the break were just 1-13 to 1-9 down, Pat Fox having scored a goal from a penalty. Fourteen minutes from time Tipperary jumped into the lead, 2-14 to 1-16, with a fine individual goal from the superb Fox. English, too, was inspirational, ending up with six points from play.

Galway, however, had not read the script and they repeated Tipp's Munster final feat of getting vital goals at the crucial stage. Corner-forward Eanna Ryan, playing the game of his life, put them back in command by firing past Ken Hogan, and then set up Noel Lane for the goal that settled it. Galway had come through 3-20 to 2-17.

There was an air of inevitability about the Galway–Tipperary rematch in 1988. Neither team brooked any serious opposition during the championship, with Galway strolling past the Offaly challenge in their semi-final match and Tipp working their way

The dynamic duo: Nicky English (left) and Pat Fox make trouble for Antrim's Terry Donnelly during the 1988 All-Ireland semi-final, which was won easily by Tipperary.

through Munster with relative ease. They had beaten Limerick easily in the Munster semi-final and led Cork by 1-12 to 0-5 at half-time in the final. A Cork rally brought them to within two points, but Tipp finished strongest and won by five points with Cormac Bonnar's goal providing the clinching score.

The feeling was that, with an extra year's experience behind them, Tipp might just edge Galway this time. Galway manager Cyril Farrell used this to his advantage, persuading his players that they hadn't been accorded the proper respect due to All-Ireland champions. Galway also had a powerful motivational force: no team from the county had ever won two All-Irelands in a row. Here was a chance to dispel the notion that Galway only won when teams from the two big provinces took their eye off the ball.

Once more, it was close, but there was to be no cigar for Tipperary. They trailed by
0-10 to 0-6 at half-time. Young Declan Ryan was wonderful at wing-forward and landed four great points, while the Tipperary defence kept a tighter rein on the dangerous Galway attackers than they had managed to the previous year. Midway through the second-half, Tipp had drawn level and would have been ahead but for a monumental save by John Commins from a fierce Pat Fox shot.

The match turned on two late goalmouth incidents. First, an English flick-on put Cormac Bonnar through, but the full-forward failed to make a proper contact and Commins managed to scramble the ball wide. Soon after, a long ball dropped between Conor O'Donovan and Galway sub. Noel Lane. Lane got the better of the duel and ran on to fire a powerful shot past Ken Hogan. His goal secured a 1-15 to 0-14 victory for Galway.

It was a deeply disappointing defeat for Tipperary, not least because neither English nor Fox had played to anything like their true form that day. Keating also received criticism for bringing on an unknown teenager, John Leahy, though Leahy's subsequent form would show that the manager had, in fact, been in the right. The match-winners for Galway had undoubtedly been their magnificent half-backs – one of the best units ever to play the game. Wing-backs Peter Finnerty and Gerry McInerney had been superb, but the star of the trio was Tony Keady in the centre. Man of the Match in the 1988 final, Keady was an awesome presence and countering his influence would be crucial if Tipp were to dethrone Galway the following year.

DOG DAYS

And that brings us to the dark and unsavoury hurling year of 1989. It is bitterly ironic that Tipp, who had played so well while losing classic games the previous two years, finally made their breakthrough in unsatisfactory circumstances. It was a throwback to the worst feature of the early years of the GAA when objections were rife and teams that won on the field lost matches in the boardroom. The Tipperary team bore no responsibility at all for this, but what was done to Galway was, not to mince words, despicable. And the man at the centre of the debacle was their star player: Tony Keady.

The role of the GAA's overseas associations is paid plentiful lip-service and often showered with praise. In fact, the GAA in New York, in particular, has never been much of a credit to the Association. In the mid-1970s, for example, there was the attempt to exercise a veto over the selection of the Dublin football team by suggesting that wing-forward David Hickey and corner-forward John McCarthy would not be welcome in New York because they had helped clear republican protesters off the pitch in Croke Park. This kind of posturing was, unfortunately, par for the course. It would have been more in the line of the New York board to properly promote Gaelic games there, but the fact was that the standard of teams there, as in London, was pitiful and that no second-generation players had emerged who had made any impact on the game.

It was the New York GAA that banjaxed Tony Keady and Galway. It had become common practice for top inter-county players to be flown out to New York to help the teams in their domestic championship – a proof of how uninterested the authorities there were in developing the game among players who actually lived in New York. Fearful that players were being paid, the GAA banned such visits by their players unless they spent a certain amount of time there before and after the game. In May 1989, Keady played a game for Laois against Tipperary in New York and was assured by officials there that he was eligible to do so. It turned out that he had, in fact, been misled and had played illegally.

BANNED FOR A YEAR

There it should have ended, as an innocent mistake, but for some never-explained reason the Games Administration Committee of the GAA decided to make an example of Keady and subsequently banned him from playing for a year. Thus, because of a pointless match in America, the 1989 All-Ireland championship was materially affected. Galway protested and threatened withdrawal from the championship, but to no avail. Five days before their semi-final match against Tipperary, their appeal to the Central Council was turned down by twenty votes to eighteen. They would not be in the best mood to defend their precious title.

It wasn't as if Tipperary hadn't had to cope with enough bad feeling already. They had completed a Munster three-in-a-row by hammering Waterford 0-26 to 2-8 in the final, but the game was best remembered for the physical approach of the losers who had two players sent off. And the stakes were raised even higher for the semi-final when Antrim pulled off their biggest shock win since the Corrigan Park miracle of 1943 by defeating Offaly 4-15 to 1-15. The winners of the second semi-final would be certainties to win the final.

Galway got off to the perfect start when Eanna Ryan scored a first-minute goal, but were then completely outplayed by Tipperary for the rest of the first-quarter, scoring no points for the next seventeen minutes. But another Ryan goal left Galway just two points down at the break and still well in it.

Tipp moved up a gear early in the second-half and a superb Fox goal put them six points clear. With the game slipping away from them, Galway seemed to lose their cool. Sylvie Linnane, a player with a reputation for on-field ferocity in the John Doyle class, pulled wildly on English and was promptly sent off. There were complaints that English had made the most of the offence and Galway railed against Wexford referee John Denton, but in vain. In his autobiography, *Beyond the Tunnel*, English admitted that he'd taken a dive. Ten minutes from time, Michael McGrath got the line. John Leahy taunted the Galwayman as he left the field and McGrath responded by clobbering Leahy with his hurl. The exchange typified the game and Tipp, even with two players more than Galway on the field, scraped through 1-17 to 2-11. You could hardly blame the players for their ill temper; the tone had been set by the administrators.

Antrim's presence in the All-Ireland final made it a novel occasion, but nobody doubted that it would rob it of any serious competitive element. Tipperary finally made the All-Ireland breakthrough by 4-24 to 3-9. The game was memorable for a bravura display of skills by English, who ended with 2-12 – a record total for an All-Ireland final. Even given the opposition, the man was breathtaking. Fox also scored a classic goal in the second-half. The other goal came in the nineteenth minute when a harmless Declan Ryan shot was fumbled to the net by Antrim keeper Niall Patterson. Once that score went in, any chance of a shock disappeared and Tipp led 1-13 to 0-5 at half-time.

The first Tipperary team in eighteen years to win the McCarthy Cup were:

Ken Hogan

John Heffernan   **Conor O'Donovan**   **Noel Sheedy**

Conal Bonnar   **Bobby Ryan**   **John Kennedy**

Colm Bonnar   **Declan Carr**

John Leahy   **Declan Ryan**   **Michael Cleary**

Pat Fox   **Cormac Bonnar**   **Nicky English**

(Subs Aidan Ryan, Joe Hayes, Donie O'Connell)

The Tipperary team that won the county's first All-Ireland in eighteen years by defeating Antrim 4-24 to 3-9 in the final at Croke Park.

With the Galway monkey finally off their back, expectations were that Tipp would build on their 1989 victory. They exuded over-confidence from the start of the 1990 season. An infamous interview in which Keating wrote off Cork's chances in the Munster Championship with the acerbic comment that 'donkeys don't win derbies' severely riled the Rebels. It seemed it riled them enough to make them play like they never had before. Accordingly, in the final, Tipp lost their crown 4-16 to 2-14. Cork's centre half-forward Mark Foley scored 2-7 from play, a feat he never remotely approached before or since. Cork went on to win the All-Ireland final and looked to have unearthed a new team of sublime quality. Their showdown with Tipperary in 1991 looked like the one to decide not only Munster honours but the destination of the All-Ireland Cup as well.

And so it proved, with the Munster final matches of that year ranking among the all-time classics. Tipperary's goose looked well cooked by the end of the first-quarter in the first match in Páirc Uí Chaoímh against Cork, as Ger Fitzgerald and John Fitzgibbon shared three goals between them. Tipp rallied and trailed by just 3-5 to 1-7 at the break thanks to a John Leahy goal and, although Fitzgibbon scored a fourth goal early in the second-half, the momentum gradually swung to the challengers. A stunning Fox goal

Opinionated, controversial, confident, but never dull, Babs Keating patrols the sideline.

Hamstrung but happy: Nicky English, who missed the game through injury, celebrates Tipperary's astonishing 4-19 to 4-15 win over Cork in the replayed 1991 Munster final.

ten minutes from time left them just four points behind and they whittled down the lead. One point down in injury time, Tipp saw English race through and once more employ his boot to steer a shot over the bar. Controversially, the umpires ruled that the ball had gone wide. A downcast English said to a reporter after the game, 'If I had ducks, they'd drown.' There would have been pandemonium at the end had Fox not popped up with a late equaliser to make it Tipp 2-16, Cork 4-10.

The replay in Thurles was even more exciting. Once more Cork got out of the blocks quicker to lead by four points at half-time and by nine points by the end of the third-quarter, a Kevin Hennessy goal leaving them 3-13 to 1-10 ahead. English had been ruled out of the game with a hamstring injury sustained during training and, ironically, the Tipp attack produced their best-ever display in the final fifteen minutes without him. With fifteen minutes left, Fox chased a long ball and flicked it past Ger Cunningham to leave just a goal between the teams. With ten minutes left an overhead flick from midfielder Declan Carr levelled the scores. The force was with Tipp.

Michael Cleary and Cormac Bonnar put them two points clear before Tomas Mulcahy shot against the post and Tipp broke for one of the great Munster final goals, Aidan Ryan charging in from the left through the Cork defenders before firing home a fierce shot. Fitzgibbon answered with a Cork goal, but two Cleary points ensured a 4-19 to 4-15 victory for Tipperary. It had been the match with everything.

TIPP'S UPS AND DOWNS

Cork complained bitterly about a pitch invasion by Tipperary supporters, which occurred during a period of Cork dominance and fatally upset their rhythm. But, as we've seen, the tactical pitch invasion had been a Cork tradition at one stage. Tipperary had loomed that lesson well and the way they played in that final quarter retrospectively dismissed any notion that they hadn't been worthy champions in 1989.

Galway were waiting for them again in the semi-final, but the great team of the late 1980s was moving over the hill now. Tipp, on the other hand, were at their very best. They led by six points at the break and won 3-13 to 1-9. So complete was their dominance that the game turned into a bit of a bore before the end. The fireworks of the past had been extinguished.

Tipp were hot favourites to beat Kilkenny in the final and not just because of their traditional Indian Sign over their neighbours. Kilkenny had struggled through each of their games and had scraped past Antrim in the semi-final by good fortune, with only two points to spare. In hindsight, expectations of a Tipperary walkover were ill-founded as Kilkenny showed their worth by winning All-Irelands in 1992 and 1993 with more or less the same team.

The Cats took the game to Tipp from the off with veteran Christy Heffernan causing havoc at centre half-forward. A Tipp defence that had been castigated for its porousness against Cork rescued the county on the day thanks to unsung heroes, like Paul Delaney, Noel Sheehy and Colm Bonnar, who all put in solid performances. It was an especially sweet day for Bonnar as his two brothers, Conal and Cormac, were also playing. Although not as spectacular as that of the Rackards, the Cashel clan's achievement was remarkable all the same. Defensive grit kept Tipp in the game in the first-half. Level at half-time, 0-9 apiece, they began to find more space in the second-half.

Still, the game's vital score had more than a touch of luck about it. Michael Cleary, whose free-taking had been incredibly accurate all year, finally mishit one ten minutes into the second-half and it skewed into the net past a wrong-footed Kilkenny defence. Tipp always had a few points to spare after that and Fox, superb all year, finished off the campaign with the insurance point that gave them a 1-16 to 0-15 victory. It was his fifth point from play in a Man of the Match performance.

Tipp actually seemed set for a couple more years of dominance after that, but these never materialised. Cork caught them at the first hurdle in 1992 and, though they regained the Munster title in 1993, a new-look Galway team beat them by 1-16 to 1-14 in the All-Ireland semi-final. It was the death knell for the side that had restored the pride of Tipperary hurling, and that was, when in full flight, one of the most attractive teams ever seen. Their depth of talent was such that two All-Ireland titles seemed a slightly miserly reward. And it's a real pity they never came up against our next team: the Clare side of the mid- to late 1990s.

All the great hurlers are, in some respect, emblematic of their era. The outlaw glint of Mick Mackey and John Doyle derived from a rough-and-ready rural way of life with its roots in the pre-modern era. Christy Ring's pioneer status and his eagerness to rush home for evening devotions on the day of a match marked him out as a typically puritan product of post-Independence Catholic Ireland. The self-confident swagger of Eamon Cregan, Babs Keating and Jimmy Barry-Murphy had a lot to do with the new prosperity of post-Lemass Ireland.

As for Nicky English, he is, in many ways, the Celtic Tiger hurler, though he had retired from the game before the era was so named. A Dublin-based investment adviser, articulate and gym-toned, he never quite won the hearts of the game's traditionalists. His play was almost too close to perfection and the clinical quality of his finishing seemed to have more to do with doing his job well than pleasing the ghosts of his forefathers. In actual fact, English is steeped in Tipperary hurling and has, for example, expressed immense admiration for John Doyle. But there always seemed to be a suspicion that he wouldn't die for the cause, that he thought too much about the game.

It was unfair, of course. You would spend a long time rewinding videos of English's career before you'd find him pulling out of a challenge. He never lacked the bottle to take on the steely Galway defence, a disappointing match in the 1988 final being balanced by sterling displays in the 1987 and 1989 semi-finals.

It's the goals, though, that marked him out as a genius. The kicked goal in the 1987 Munster final, the fluid lift-and-strike in the replay that year, the shot on the run that completed his remarkable 2-12 tally in the 1989 All-Ireland final: they were goals you couldn't imagine any other player of his era scoring.

Soon after quitting the game in 1996, English was back as Tipperary manager. He steered the county to their first All-Ireland win in 2001 – their first since 1991 – just when there were murmurs that another famine might be taking hold. That Tipp team came out on top in a series of tight finishes, greatly helped by the calmness of a manager who kept his head when all around were losing theirs. Once again, his coolness under pressure proved to be his greatest attribute.

Without that English *sangfroid,* there might not have been a Tipp revival. In the 1987 Munster final it was the Lattin-Cullen man who took on the responsibility in the last second in Thurles. Tipp, a point down, looked set to reassume the mantle of gallant losers, until English got hold of the ball and forced a free from which Pat Fox struck the equaliser. They were a point down in the replay in Killarney when English again got on the ball, racing clear of the Cork defence, sizing up his options and handpassing the ball over the bar to bring the game into extra time. In that immortal GAA phrase, 'The right man had it.'

THE REVOLUTIONARIES

Clare, 1995–1998

Munster Champions 1995, 1997, 1998

All-Ireland Champions 1995, 1997

There is no more intriguing story in this book than that of Clare hurling in the second half of the last decade. In fact, you could argue that there's no more interesting story in Irish sport. It took just four years for Clare to emerge from anonymity to become the team everyone had an opinion on. Has there ever been a sporting event as emotional as the Munster final of 1995 when Clare made the breakthrough after sixty-three years in the wilderness? Or as unlikely a victory as their eventual triumph in that year's All-Ireland final? Or as controversial a hurling year as 1998? Clare started the 1990s as the team nobody knew, became the team everyone loved and ended the decade as the team hated by a large proportion of the country's hurling followers. What's more, every single match they played was an event.

The special flavour of this Clare team was largely due to one man. We left Ger Loughnane beating his fists on the unyielding Thurles ground on 30 July 1978. He was grieving the knowledge that the finest Clare team in nearly fifty years would never win a Munster title. It was a poignant sight and the years had made those 1977 and 1978 losses even more resonant. Clare had come no closer since and, by the 1990s, it seemed almost incredible that they had ever come so close.

When Loughnane then took over as team manager in September 1994, the belief that Clare would never again win a Munster title had solidified into an immutable law. This was referred to by some as 'Biddy Early's Curse', although the fact that the Clare wise woman had died long before the GAA was founded should probably exempt her from blame. They had been humiliated by Tipperary in the 1993 Munster final and then by Limerick in the 1994 final. Clare, as always, seemed up to an upset, but incapable of stringing two good results together.

Hindsight can tempt people to underplay the enormity of Clare's achievement. True, they had players who would have been great in any era, for example, Davey Fitzgerald in goal, Brian Lohan at full-back, Sean McMahon at centre half-back and Jamesie O'Connor at midfield and wing-forward. Colin Lynch and Ollie Baker were to become the finest midfield pairing of the decade; Anthony Daly developed into one of hurling's great leaders; Ger O'Loughlin provided important scores at vital times. All the same, Clare had fewer outstanding individuals than most teams that win more than a single All-Ireland. What made them great was the power of the team as a unit and the impetus provided by Loughnane's guile as a manager and motivator, along with the superb physical conditioning inculcated by their severely underrated trainer, Mike McNamara.

LOUGHNANE'S PREDICTION

There were some signs of the surprises to come when Clare reached the 1995 League final, but they were once more relegated in most people's minds to their usual status of also-rans when they were hammered by Kilkenny. Loughnane did predict that Clare would recover and win the Munster Championship, but no one believed him. No one, it turned out, except his players.

The game that set the show on the road was that year's Munster semi-final. It didn't look epochal at the time, but it contained so many mythic overtones, so many proofs that Clare could overcome any adversity that, in hindsight, it was the perfect scene-setter for what was to follow. A meagre 14,000 fans were in Limerick that day and the scepticism of the long-suffering Banner followers seemed to be borne out when Cork led by four points at half-time, despite having played against the wind.

Early in the second-half, Cork stretched that lead to seven points, aided by the terrible shooting of the Clare forwards who ended the match with an incredible twenty wides. Clare hung in grimly, but suffered a further blow when Sean McMahon broke his collar bone. All of their subs had already been used, so Clare were forced to keep McMahon on the pitch. Showing incredible bravery, he played on, one-handed, in the right corner of the attack.

With five minutes left on the clock, Clare were still three points down. Then Ger O'Loughlin scored a goal and a point from PJ O'Connell seemed to have secured an unlikely win for the outsiders. The fat lady hadn't sung just yet, however. On the stroke of normal time a Kevin Murray goal for Cork put the Rebels two points ahead. That seemed to be that for Clare, but in injury time the one-armed McMahon forced Timmy

The Clare team that defeated Cork in the Munster championship semi-final 1997.

Kelleher to concede a sideline ball. Fergus Touhy floated the line-ball into the goalmouth and Ollie Baker flicked it to the net.

The fun wasn't over yet though. Alan Browne had a chance to bring the game to a replay, but his shot came off the post. It dropped to Ger Manley who was in front of goal and unmarked, but Frank Lohan appeared as if from nowhere to block his shot and change the course of hurling history.

All the late dramatics could not completely mask the fact that it had been a poor game, and Clare were expected to complete their own kind of three-in-a-row by receiving a third consecutive Munster final trouncing when they met Limerick in Thurles. Limerick had been desperately unlucky not to win the All-Ireland the year before – somehow managing to concede 2-5 in the last five minutes of the game when they had been five points clear of Offaly. So they were angry, experienced, had stuffed Clare the year before and in centre half-back Ciaran Carey had an inspirational star and leader.

DAVEY FITZ'S LEAP

But this was the day when Loughnane's side did what the fine team of 1977 and 1978 had not been able to do. Limerick moved into an early 0-5 to 0-2 lead, but this time they couldn't get away. Five minutes before the break, Clare were awarded a penalty and goalie Davey Fitzgerald came all the way upfield to take it, wielding a hurley with a *bos* of frying-pan proportions. The three men on the line never saw the shot and Fitzgerald even had time for a celebratory leap as he sprinted back to his goal. Clare were 1-6 to 0-7 up at half-time and, at last, their fans began to believe.

In fact, Clare made history that day with something to spare, running Limerick off their feet in the second-half to win 1-17 to 0-11. Symptomatic of their dominance was PJ O'Connell's destruction of Ciaran Carey, who was previously seen as entirely indestructible. O'Connell had been written off as an obsessive solo-runner of limited effectiveness. His long hair, moustache and suntan made him look like a 'Miami Vice' villain, and he was never going to win any prizes for stylish hurling. Yet here he was, outpacing Carey to every ball, landing a succession of great points and winning the Man of the Match award. The penny dropped: there was more to O'Connell and his team-mates than met the eye.

Clare had also benefitted from repeating the crafty trick Limerick had used in the 1936 Munster final. Back then Mick Mackey had played with a bandage on his uninjured knee, this time Sean McMahon's healthy shoulder was strapped up. And although they had patented the ruse so many years before, Limerick never suspected and wasted time testing the wrong shoulder.

A familiar sight as Ger Loughnane acclaims victory with the fans.

The magnificent Brian Lohan bursting clear, in typical style, from Pádraig Tobin of Limerick.

The joy in Clare was such that the team took the provincial trophy on a tour of the county, something normally reserved for All-Ireland winning teams. Their tour of triumph fuelled the view that Clare had achieved their goal for the season, and Galway were fancied to dispose of them in the All-Ireland semi-final. So much for predictions! Clare led by 2-6 to 0-7 at half-time and added a third goal early in the second-half thanks to Ger O'Loughlin who, along with Conor Clancy, tortured the Galway full-back line throughout. Galway replied with a Francis Forde goal and Clare listed briefly before long-range points from O'Connell and outstanding right half-back Liam Doyle put them on an even keel again. In the end, the 3-12 to 1-13 win was an easy one. And so Clare was once more back in the major league, ready to face Offaly in the All-Ireland final.

Offaly, it was now believed, would be a different matter with no easy scores available. The reigning All-Ireland champions looked an even better team this term. They had given one of the outstanding displays of the decade when defeating Kilkenny 2-16 to 2-5 in the Leinster final, a win even more comprehensive than that scoreline suggests as the two Kilkenny goals came in the closing minutes. Tradition was even more firmly against Clare than it had been in the Munster final as their only previous All-Ireland title had been in 1914. That victory had been secured by a team trained by Jim O'Hehir, father of the legendary RTÉ commentator, Michael.

THE MOULD CRACKS

But from the outset you could hear the mould cracking under the weight of Clare's persistence. From early in the game it was obvious that Clare weren't going to give Offaly a chance to repeat the flowing hurling that had destroyed Kilkenny. The remarkable fitness of Clare and the exceptional quality of their back-line denied Offaly space, although it seemed the outsiders had suffered a severe blow just before half-time when the normally flawless Fitzgerald fumbled a Michael Duignan cross into the net. Clare, vitally, replied with two points before half-time to trail by just 1-6 to 0-7 at the break.

The second-half was an equally tight affair. Brian Lohan was magnificent at full-back for Clare, despite having to play the final twenty minutes with a torn hamstring. So well did he play that Offaly never suspected that the Clare full-back was in such dire straits. Clare were having problems up front, though, as Jamesie O'Connor – so magnificent against Cork, Limerick and Galway – hit a rare off-day. When Johnny Pilkington scored a second Offaly goal fifteen minutes from time, it looked as though Offaly might stretch the margin far enough.

Clare, however, refused to give up. Touhy was having the game of his life and shot four crucial points from play. For all that, they were still 2-7 to 0-11 behind with just four minutes left to create a miracle. It was time for a little-known substitute, Eamonn Taaffe, to make his name.

The happiest days of your life: Banner captain Anthony Daly is chaired from the field after Clare's stunning 1995 All-Ireland final win over Offaly.

Taaffe hadn't even gotten on the field in the Munster final, and it's fair to say that he had been having a miserable time since being brought on as a sub. for Steven McNamara. In fact, he'd been doing so badly that Loughnane was preparing to replace him with Alan Neville and had already written out the necessary document for the referee. But then Daly's long free reached the Offaly goalmouth. Taaffe first-timed the ball to the net to put Clare a point ahead. Johnny Dooley levelled almost immediately, but it was clear the tide had turned in Clare's favour. They forced a sixty-five and Anthony Daly elected to take it instead of Sean McMahon. It was an inspired decision. Daly was better under pressure and he duly struck the ball over the bar. A close-range free from O'Connor soon after gave Clare a 1-13 to 2-8 victory and concluded one of the most unexpected championship campaigns of all time.

Clare had come from nowhere to become one of the most popular teams ever to win the championship. Their determination, guts and strength of character as a team inspired the nation. That September, people who weren't from Clare wished they were. It had been a once-in-a-lifetime season.

David Fitzgerald

Michael O'Halloran   **Brian Lohan**   **Frank Lohan**

Liam Doyle   **Sean McMahon**   **Anthony Daly**

Jamesie O'Connor   **Ollie Baker**

Fergus Touhy   **PJ O'Connell**   **Fergal Hegarty**

Steven McNamara   **Conor Clancy**   **Ger O'Loughlin**

(Subs Eamonn Taaffe, Cyril Lyons, Alan Neville)

A LONG WAY TO GO

Clare gave up their crown first time out the following year, playing well but losing by one point to Limerick. The winning score was a magnificent individual effort from a back-on-form Ciaran Carey. Still, they weren't forgotten. Wexford were that year's unlikely All-Ireland champions, their resurgence partly credited to the example Clare had set the year before. This wasn't a revolt, it was a revolution.

That defeat by Limerick might have spelled the end for Clare. They had won their All-Ireland and the consensus was that although they had seized their opportunity, they weren't really a team of the first rank. After all, beating Limerick, Galway and Offaly to win the championship wasn't the same as cutting a swathe through the traditional Big Three of hurling. As far as hurling was concerned, Clare still had a lot to prove.

The following year, 1997, would be the year that Clare would complete the transformation from being a good team to being a great team. The matches they played were of better quality than those they had played two years earlier and they had to defeat Cork, Kilkenny and Tipperary on their way to the title. Only one other team had previously done that – the 1959 Waterford team – and Clare bettered them by throwing in a second victory over Tipp for good measure. But it wasn't plain sailing. Yet again there were cliff-hangers, red herrings and Hollywood endings.

The championship season began with a stroke of luck for Clare. Loughnane had opted not to give midfielder Colin Lynch his debut against Cork in the Munster semi-final. Lynch, according to his manager, was far from gruntled and felt he'd been unfairly treated. However, ill feeling had no chance to develop between the two men. Fergal Hegarty was forced to pull out of the Cork game with an injury and Lynch was on the team. He played brilliantly and by the end of the year was one half of the best midfield

One time 'Miami Vice'-villain lookalike and fine forward PJ O'Connell scores Clare's second goal in the replayed All-Ireland quarter-final of 1999 against Galway.

pairing in the game. The other half was Ollie Baker, a hard-working journeyman in 1995 who became an all-round hurler in 1997. Baker's duckling-to-swan metamorphosis was symptomatic of a change in Clare generally. This time around self-belief and team spirit were buttressed by a considerable amount of skill.

For all that, they got it tough enough from a young Cork side whose right half-forward, Seanie McGrath, gave Anthony Daly an unaccustomed runaround. The match was in doubt until the closing minutes when O'Loughlin put McNamara through for a goal and sealed a 1-19 to 0-18 victory. That score was a tribute to the immense courage and high pain threshold of O'Loughlin: just before he made the pass, he'd received a tremendous whack in the testicles from his marker's hurley. He still provided the perfect assist before falling to the ground in agony. Afterwards in the dressing room, when he was asked about the injury, he quipped, 'I felt I had to come off and count them.'

CLARE EARNS RESPECT

That year's Munster final in Páirc Uí Chaoímh is the one Loughnane remembers as his favourite match. It was, he said after the game, a day when Clare earned respect. Beating Limerick in a Munster decider was one thing, but defeating Tipp, who had put the Banner to the sword so often, was another thing entirely. An extra frisson was added by the fact that Len Gaynor, who had managed most of the Clare players before Loughnane took over, was in charge of Tipperary. There was also the fact that the Clare players held bitter memories of an incident in the 1993 final when they felt Nicky English had laughed at them while scoring late in the game. The incident might not have happened at all, but it was a powerful motivational tool for their manager.

The game was agonisingly, breathtakingly, heartbreakingly close. Clare played superb hurling in the first-half with Brian Lohan giving one of the great Munster final full-back performances against the dangerous Michael Cleary. They led by 0-13 to 0-8 at the break, but seven minutes into the second-half Tipperary had drawn level and looked to be on fire. Clare went back ahead with a long free from Sean McMahon and it was nip-and-tuck all the way after that. Once more, though, the Banner came up with the crucial goal at the crucial moment, young David Forde cutting in and striking a tremendous shot to the net. They won 1-18 to 0-18 and were now warm favourites for their second All-Ireland title in three years. The victory, though, had been in doubt right until the very end: in the last minute John Leahy, Tipp's star player, found himself unmarked in front of goal, but mishit his shot. Tipp had missed their chance. However, the new back-door system introduced by the GAA, whereby defeated provincial finalists got back into the competition in operation, meant there was every chance that Tipperary, and Leahy, would get another crack at Clare.

In the All-Ireland semi-final, Clare had the opportunity to complete their clean sweep over the Big Three. Kilkenny had lost the Leinster final to Wexford but had won the All-Ireland quarter-final against Galway, thanks to a phenomenal display by DJ Carey. Carey – the closest thing the modern era had to a Ring, or a Mackey – had never played better than when racking up 2-8 against the westerners. Clare knew he had the potential to negate their undoubted edge over Kilkenny.

The battle between Carey and the Clare defence ended honours even. He looked devastatingly sharp on the day, but was superbly marked, while David Fitzgerald made a fantastic save from a Carey penalty. Carey did score a wonderful goal in the final quarter, but by then the game had gone beyond Kilkenny. Clare led 1-16 to 0-8 going into the last quarter, and though that goal prompted a furious and typical revival from the Kilkennymen, Clare were very good value for their 1-17 to 1-13 win.

Clare also proved that they had a major star forward of their own in Jamesie O'Connor, who had the game of his life, firing over five impressive points from play. Unsung grafter Conor Clancy also played a major role, moving to centre half-forward and preventing Kilkenny's Number Six, Pat O'Neill, from exerting his usual dominance.

Tipp waited in the final, having pulverised reigning champions Wexford in the other semi. They looked to have come on since the Munster decider and Loughnane was faced with an unenviable task. Clare had already produced a massive effort to beat Tipperary once before, and all the pressure was on them again. If they lost the final, not only would they have that defeat to contend with but their Munster final victory would be tarnished. Psychologically, Tipp held all the aces. They were fired up by what they had regarded as unnecessary Clare triumphalism after the Munster final. Anthony Daly's post-match speech, in which he asserted that Clare were 'no longer the whipping boys in Munster', had rubbed a lot of people up the wrong way. Tipp were out to prove a point.

REACHING THE ZENITH

The 1997 final was the high water mark for this Clare side. It was also one of the best games of the decade. Tipperary had a good breeze behind them in the first-half, but struggled to find their groove and led only 0-3 to 0-2 after the first-quarter. Then Declan Ryan and John Leahy began to pick off points and by the twenty-fifth minute they were five points clear and set fair to build a match-winning lead by half-time.

Clare rallied, however, and one brilliant two-minute spell yielded three points. Two of these came from Niall Gilligan, the Sixmilebridge youngster playing in his first final, who was giving an unexpected roasting to Paul Shelley, the outstanding defender in the game that year. At half-time Tipperary were 0-10 to 0-6 ahead. It didn't look to be quite enough.

Jest in Time: a young fan rushes to congratulate Brian Lohan after Clare's victory in the 1997 All-Ireland final against Tipperary.

Within fifteen seconds of the restart, Liam Doyle, the most underrated defender in the game, had sent over a great point. Four Clare points followed in quick succession within the next six minutes, and a Colin Lynch score made it 0-11 each. Another Banner youngster now emerged to play a major role. Forde, the goal hero in the Munster final, had been brought on ostensibly as a right corner-forward, but he proceeded to roam all over the attack. The decision by his marker, Michael Ryan, not to follow him proved to be a fatal miscalculation. Forde scored two points and set up one more to leave Clare 0-17 to 0-12 up with just over ten minutes left on the clock.

Clare were going so well at this stage that it looked as though, for once, they'd have the game wrapped up well before the final whistle. But as usual there were a few more twists in store before the referee could call it a day. Sub. Liam Cahill put Tipp back in the game with an opportunist goal, and four minutes from time teenager Eugene O'Neill doubled on a free that had come back off the crossbar and found the net. It was 2-13 to 0-18 for Tipp, and Clare faced their biggest challenge ever.

Ollie Baker, colossal throughout, levelled with a massive point and then Lynch found O'Connor on the right, fifty yards from goal. O'Connor's shot flew over the bar and landed in the hand of Ger Loughnane who had gone behind the goal to relay instructions to his forwards. You couldn't have made it up. That would have been a dramatic enough finale, but there was yet more to come. A great pass from Brian O'Meara found Leahy in front of the Clare goal, in almost exactly the same position he'd taken up in the last minute of the Munster final. He could have taken his point and clinched a replay, but instead he went for broke. Fitzgerald brilliantly saved the low shot and Tipp were sunk.

THE PUBLIC'S FAVOURITE

At that point, Clare's stock was never higher and they were the people's favourite. But that was about to change. The downturn in the public's perception of the team perhaps began that night when RTÉ broadcast the team's victory banquet. The comments of the 'Sunday Game' panel, made directly after the match, were relayed to the revellers and Loughnane felt that Eamon Cregan had been begrudging about Clare's victory. When Loughnane was subsequently interviewed he began by saying, 'After listening to that ten-minute whinge from Eamon Cregan ...' and he went on from there. There may have been a real grievance behind this attack, but it came across as mean-spirited and paranoid at a time when Clare could afford to be generous. Added to the Daly 'whipping boys no longer' speech and incidents when Loughnane had engaged in a slanging match with Tipperary County Board official Liz Howard and had appeared to cast aspersions on Len Gaynor's management skills, it all left a sour taste in the mouth. And so it was that the Irish sports-loving public began to fall out of love with Clare, though outright hatred hadn't set in yet.

For all that, no one doubted that Clare would retain their All-Ireland title in 1998. This belief was reinforced when they outclassed Cork in the Munster semi-final, defeating the reigning National League champions by 0-21 to 0-14. So it was very surprising when they were held to a draw in the Munster final by Waterford. Clare looked as though they had been caught napping as Waterford drew level with late scores. And there was a sharp intake of breath as Paul Flynn missed a long free that would have clinched the game for unfancied Waterford. Clare remained favourites for the replay, but no one expected what actually did transpire.

INTIMIDATIONS AND ALLEGATIONS

Loughnane's autobiography, *Raising the Banner*, suggests that Clare went into the game nursing a fierce grudge against the Waterford team because they felt they had been physically intimidated in the first match. Yet my own memory of the first, drawn game is that it hadn't been particularly rough at all. The second match, however, would make up for that.

Before the *sliothar* had even been thrown in, a fired-up Colin Lynch was pulling recklessly across Peter Queally and Tony Browne at midfield, and two minutes into the match Brian Lohan and Michael White came to blows in front of the Clare goal. Then several players got involved in a mêlée and Lynch decked Browne. Referee Willie Barrett restored order by sending off Lohan and White, while Lynch was lucky to get away with a booking. The rest of the match was played in exceedingly bad spirit, but Clare, who had been just 0-7 to 0-5 up at the break, pulled away to win 2-16 to 0-10 with the goals coming from Clancy and Gilligan.

That's when things started to get seriously nutty. Whatever the rights and wrongs of Clare's macho approach in the replay, the RTÉ Radio 'Sportscall' programme on the following Monday was a triumph of hype over common sense. In between suggestions that Clare had brought rough play to a new level came allegations that a Clare player was on steroids and that Loughnane, a teacher by profession, was not fit to do his job. But it was the hue and cry over rough play that was to have the biggest repercussions. Lynch, it seemed, was about to be lynched.

Banished to the stands, Clare manager Ger Loughnane and selector Tony Considine contemplate their plans during the 1998 All-Ireland semi-final against Offaly.

Looking back at the whole affair now, it seems almost unreal. The Munster Council suspended Lynch for three months, a move many regarded as a reaction to public outcry. It sparked a litany of unsavoury events: Clare announced that they would be 'retiring' the Number Three jersey in their next game when Lohan was suspended; there were unsubstantiated claims by the Clare County Chairman Robert Frost that he had overheard a conversation between three mysterious priests who knew what suspension Lynch would get before the Munster Council had even met; Loughnane made a statement alleging that the Council was run by a shadowy figure who could be compared to Don Corleone; and Clare people waited vigilantly outside a midnight meeting of the Council as Lynch's fate was decided. Clare may have been dealt with harshly, but they'd let common sense go out the window. In doing so, they probably cost themselves a championship they had been almost certain to win.

Minus Lohan and Lynch, and obviously distracted by the post-Munster final circus, Clare played poorly against Offaly in the All-Ireland semi-final. They should have done better. Offaly had played dreadfully while losing the Leinster final to Kilkenny, and their manager, Babs Keating, had responded by comparing them to 'sheep in a heap'. As a result, the players staged a dramatic dressing-room *coup*, which ousted Keating and installed the unknown Michael Bond as their new manager. Despite all this, Offaly still put up a spirited display against Clare, and it took a late equalising point from Jamesie O'Connor to earn the hot favourites a 1-13-all draw. The champions, however, were back on form for the replay and can seldom have been more impressive than they were in the first-half when they tore apart the Offaly defence, with new wing-forward Alan Markham giving the great Brian Whelehan the runaround. Clare led comfortably for most of the match and, even after a determined Offaly fight back late in the game, were still 1-16 to 2-10 up with two minutes left.

It was then that Fate swaggered into the stadium with the final cruel trick she had been waiting to play on Clare. Referee Jimmy Cooney blew the final whistle with those two minutes left on the clock and he was ushered from the pitch by unsuspecting officials before he could correct his mistake. Clare celebrated wildly, but the result was never going to be allowed to stand, especially after Offaly fans invaded and occupied the Croke Park pitch in protest. Had Cooney not made that mistake, it seems likely that Clare would have won and gone on to take a second All-Ireland in a row.

C H A N G I N G   F O R T U N E S

As it was, they were forced into a third match against Offaly the following Saturday. By now Clare looked exhausted from their run of matches and controversy, while Offaly, the most naturally talented but least physically diligent hurlers in the country, had benefitted hugely from their two extra games. There was nothing more in the tank for Loughnane's side. Veteran Joe Dooley scored five great points from play, and keeper Steven Byrne made a trinity of wonderful saves. Offaly won by 0-16 to 0-13.

Clare were never the same after 1998. They reached the Munster final in 1999, but lost to Cork and were knocked out in the All-Ireland semi-final by Kilkenny. An opening-round defeat in Munster the year after spelled the end of the great team, though more than half the players still ply their trade at inter-county level. They had been miracle-workers. And even if their story had ended on a sour note, they had still created more interest in hurling than any other team in living memory. You couldn't but love them in 1995. And after 1998 admiration was still the only proper response, even if a story that had begun like *Finian's Rainbow* wound up like *The Godfather*.

There is, however, an intriguing afterword to the Clare story, which developed just as we were putting this book to bed. Wins over Galway, by 0-16 to 1-12 in the All-Ireland quarter-final, and over Waterford, by 1-15 to 1-12 in the semi-final, put them back into the All-Ireland final against Kilkenny, where they gave a good account of themselves before losing 2-20 to 0-19 to exceptional opposition. It was an outcome no one would have forecast at the start of the year when Tipperary beat them in the Munster Championship. This time around, however, the back-door had worked in Clare's favour.

Maybe it's stretching it a bit to say that this belongs in the same chapter as the victories of 1995 and 1997. Four years have gone by since the crazy summer of 1998 and Ger Loughnane has been replaced as manager by Cyril Lyons. But the fact remains that over half of the current team played in the 1997 final, and the driving forces behind this revival are the familiar figures of Frank Lohan, Sean McMahon, Jamesie O'Connor, Colin Lynch and, above all, the semi-final Man of the Match Brian Lohan. There's no doubt that the heroics of 2002 are a kind of epilogue to the story begun by Ger Loughnane's men in that 1995 Munster semi-final against Cork.

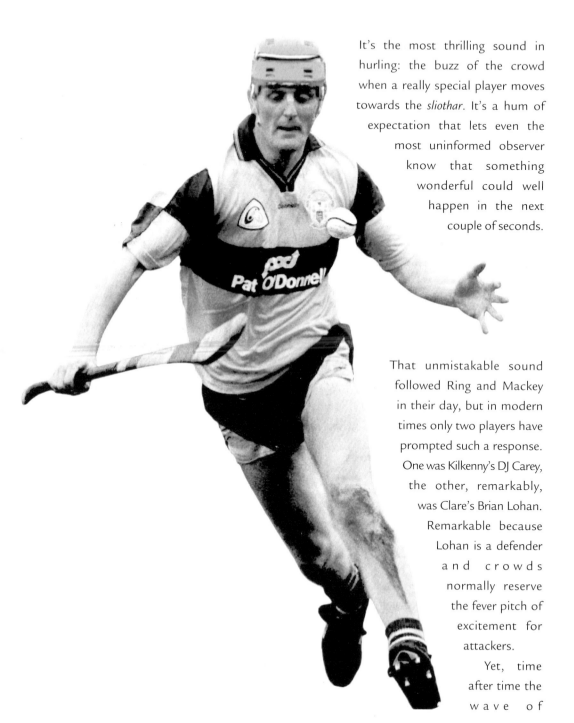

It's the most thrilling sound in hurling: the buzz of the crowd when a really special player moves towards the *sliothar*. It's a hum of expectation that lets even the most uninformed observer know that something wonderful could well happen in the next couple of seconds.

That unmistakable sound followed Ring and Mackey in their day, but in modern times only two players have prompted such a response. One was Kilkenny's DJ Carey, the other, remarkably, was Clare's Brian Lohan. Remarkable because Lohan is a defender and crowds normally reserve the fever pitch of excitement for attackers.

Yet, time after time the wave of

audible excitement would ripple through the Banner fans when the *sliothar* went in Lohan's direction. They knew that the man in the red helmet would get to the ball first, and that when surrounded by the opposition he would use his speed and strength and intelligence to get out of an impossible position and make room for a clearance way down the field.

In Lohan's hands, full-back play became a vehicle for the kind of expressiveness normally denied to defenders. Caution seemed alien to the man when he embarked on those clearing missions. There were times when he could have passed the ball to a colleague or lain down in expectation of a free, but instead he seemed to welcome the tackles and the fouls. He seemed delighted with the chance to prove his worth and always played with the certainty that he would cut the ball out and make that clearance. He must have done it a hundred times in Clare's glory years.

Lohan seemed a quintessential Clareman, but he and his brother Frank could have ended up in Galway jerseys had their father, Gus, not moved south from his native county and become a team-mate of Ger Loughnane's on the so-near-and-yet-so-far Banner team of the 1970s. The feats of his sons made Gus the most influential Galway exile since Tony Reddan had decamped to Lorrha.

We became so used to regarding Lohan as invincible that players who got any change whatsoever out of him were regarded as having proved themselves major figures of the sport. Eugene O'Neill took 1-1 off him in the 1997 All-Ireland final and was rewarded with a Young Player of the Year award, though the goal had been a fortuitous rebound that Lohan could do nothing about. When a teenage Eugene Cloonan managed two points off the Clare full-back in the All-Ireland club final between Athenry and Wolfe Tones, he was named Man of the Match.

Some of Lohan's team-mates from the 1995 to 1998 vintage have never reached the same heights again. The man himself is just as awesome. In this year's All-Ireland semi-final against Waterford, he was flawless, winning the Man of the Match award as he inspired his side to an upset win over the Munster champions. There he was, doing it again: racing onto the loose *sliothar*, defying the attackers and launching it back to where it came from. The crowd buzzed again when he did it. Lohan's story is not yet finished. He may be great again. And even if he's not, he will always be regarded as one of the very best – a living proof that all the legends do not belong to the past.

THE REJUVENATORS

Waterford, 2002

Munster Champions 2002

Waterford's 2002 victory came at a time when people were beginning to wonder if the Munster hurling final had lost its old magic, if, indeed, it really mattered anymore. The 'backdoor system', in place since 1997, meant that a team could lose a Munster decider and still remain in the championship. As a result, the games seemed to have lost the all-or-nothing quality which had made them so visceral. Provincial deciders, in both football and hurling, had become anachronistic because of the emphasis on the All-Ireland series and the suggestion that nothing else was important. Cork may have defeated Tipperary in a wonderful final in 2000, but their All-Ireland semi-final loss to Offaly saw them tagged as abject failures. In short, the Munster hurling final seemed to have become just another game.

Waterford changed all that when they won their first provincial title in thirty-nine years in magnificent style, defeating Tipperary 2-23 to 3-12 at Páirc Uí Chaoimh, in a game that ranks with any of the great finals you care to mention. The outpouring of raw emotion from the Waterford fans at the final whistle showed just how much this victory meant to them. The Munster Championship had been rejuvenated.

The Decies had gone into that game as rank outsiders against the reigning All-Ireland champions, who had approached perfection when ruthlessly dismantling Limerick in the semi-final. But then, they had also been outsiders against Cork in the provincial semi-final in Thurles, which they won 1-16 to 1-15. Waterford's legendary victory against Cork was largely due to the brilliant Paul Flynn, who kept them in touch throughout with a string of long-range points from frees and from play. And when, in

the second-half, a long delivery from Tony Browne somehow eluded the normally
reliable Cork keeper Donal Óg Cusack and ended up in the back of the net, they must
have realised it was going to be their day. Ken McGrath, hampered by an injury and only
brought on late as a sub, shot the winning point in a frenetic finish.

Nonetheless, on Munster final day, Tipperary were hotter-than-hot favourites and began
as though they would sweep Waterford off the field, leading 0-6 to 0-2 after just ten minutes.
The catalyst for the Waterford revival was a superb piece of opportunism from Flynn, who
expertly found the net from a twenty-one-yard free. Eoghan Kelly repeated the feat for Tipp
on the stroke of half-time, but the champions were just 1-10 to 1-9 up after playing with a
strong wind at their backs. Waterford were poised at the threshold, but would they have the
bottle to finish the job?

The chances didn't look too good when Benny Dunne scored a goal for Tipperary
just after the restart, but Waterford responded superbly with five fine points in a row.
Dunne answered with another goal and the sides were level. Both teams knew the next
goal would be crucial, and it was Waterford who got it – seventeen minutes into the
second-half – as Tony Browne raced onto a long clearance and slipped the ball past
Brendan Cummins. From then on it was exhibition stuff as Waterford picked off a
string of points to run out easy winners. Ken McGrath gave one of the great Munster
final performances, bagging seven points from play; John Mullane and Eoin Kelly
tormented the Tipp defence and got seven more between them; Tony Browne ruled
midfield; and Fergal Hartley was imperious at centre half-back.

The commanding Fergal Hartley plucks the ball from over the head of Tipperary's Conor Gleeson.

It was notable how many echoes of past Munster finals attended this recent triumph. Waterford's clinching second goal, for example, was swept in by Tony Browne, whose tussle with Colin Lynch in 1998 had caused all the crazy controversy that year. The Tipperary team were managed by Nicky English, who himself had provided so many exquisite, memorable final moments. English's old team-mate, Colm Bonnar, had switched sides since their days on the turf and was there now as a Waterford mentor. And when Fergal Hartley hoisted the cup over his head, he had good-naturedly echoed Richard Stakelum's famous 1987 victory speech by declaring, 'The *real* famine is over.'

Most poignant of all was the role of Justin McCarthy as Waterford manager. A quarter of a century had passed since he had brought another success-starved county, Clare, to a Munster final and had seen them heartbreakingly denied two years in a row. At that time, his shot at managerial glory seemed to have been comprehensively denied, and even within the county of Waterford there had been rumbles of discontent at his appointment as manager of the county team after they were knocked out of the 2001 championship. Now McCarthy had proven that he was still a manager of the first rank, that he could still get the best out of players who had been written off by those who couldn't see beyond the Big Two of Cork and Tipperary.

On the Thursday before the final, McCarthy brought in three of the greatest Waterford hurlers of all time – Martin Óg Morrissey, Tom Cheasty and Frankie Walsh of the 1957,

Eoghan McGrath shows the kind of determination needed to win a Munster title as he breaks away from the challenge of Tipperary's Tom Costello.

1959 and 1963 teams respectively – to talk to his team. He said afterwards that he regarded this as the pivotal moment in their preparations, the encounter that made all the difference on the day of the final. McCarthy understood well that in Munster hurling, history matters.

Unfortunately, Waterford were unable to complete the fairytale by capturing the Liam McCarthy Cup as well. In the semi-final against a Clare team that had returned through 'the back door', the new Munster champions looked like they had been totally drained by the enormity of bridging that thirty-nine-year gap. Flynn scored another goal from a twenty-one-yard free and young Eoghan Kelly's performance was good enough to secure him an All-Star award, but the Banner looked better focussed throughout, a fact reflected in the final score of 1-15 to 1-12.

But 2002 will still stand as one of the great years for Waterford hurling. After humiliation in 1982 and 1983, controversy in 1998 and innumerable other disappointing defeats, they had returned as a force to be reckoned with in Munster hurling, showing that they could not be dismissed, that today's men in white are worthy heirs to the great stars of the past.

The 2002 Waterford team were:

Steven Brenner

James Murray   **Tom Feeney**   **Brian Flannery**

Eoghan Murphy   **Fergal Hartley**   **Brian Greene**

Tony Browne   **Peter Queally**

Ken McGrath   **Paul Flynn**   **Eoghan Kelly**

Eoghan McGrath   **Seamus Prendergast**   **John Mullane**

Subs: D. Bennett, M. White, A. Moloney, D. Shanahan

A sports psychologist once put forward the theory that there were sound empirical reasons why a few counties dominate the GAA while the other counties struggle perennially to overcome tradition. Think of it, he said, like this: the young lad from the weaker county travels to matches in his childhood, sees his team hammered and listens to the lamentations of the grown-ups on the way home. He comes to think that this is the way things are. When he grows up and takes on the powerful counties on the pitch, he's subconsciously convinced of his inferiority. Which is all well and good, but Ken McGrath would seem to provide incontrovertible proof that the theory is fallacious. If it were true, he could be excused for becoming a quivering nervous wreck every time he plays against Cork, whereas he has in fact consistently tormented the Rebels' defence, as he has that of every other county he's come up against during his short inter-county career.

Ken is the son of Pat McGrath, a stylish defender of considerable talent who had the misfortune to be on the Waterford side that was destroyed by Cork in the 1982 Munster final.

That was probably the greatest humiliation ever suffered by a team in the provincial decider, and it obscured the fact that Pat McGrath and his team-mates were a good side that didn't deserve to be remembered for one bad day out. It was to be another twenty years before Waterford finally erased their reputation as Munster final chokers, and no one did more to help them smash the tradition of inferiority and secure that historic victory over Tipperary than Ken McGrath, with a stunning haul of seven points.

McGrath was tipped for stardom from early on. A teenage prodigy, he achieved the incredible feat of playing for the Minor, under-21 and Senior Waterford teams in one year (1996), and looked a good senior into the bargain. Strong, quick, accurate and absolutely fearless, he was the latest in a line of great forwards to come out of the marvellous Mount Sion club. Over the next few years he earned a reputation as one of the best attackers in the game, even if the Decies still weren't able to break through.

It looked initially as though 2002, far from being McGrath's greatest year, would be a complete washout. Waterford were drawn against a Cork side that had recently lost to Kilkenny by just a point in the National League final. They were unfancied and their odds lengthened when injury forced McGrath out of the starting line-up. But Waterford hung on doggedly for most of the game and McGrath was sprung from the bench. Obviously hampered, he was still there to shoot the winning point and propel the county into the provincial final.

The performance he gave against Tipperary in that unforgettable final is already legendary, and he closed out the year by scoring eleven points for Mount Sion as they beat old rivals Ballygunner in the county final. He also scooped Man of the Match honours when Mount Sion won the Munster club title.

McGrath looks sure to be one of the stars of the new millennium, although Tipperary's Eoghan Kelly, Cork's Joe Deane and Limerick's Andrew O'Shaughnessy will challenge him for pre-eminence in the province. By his side will be younger brother Eoghan, who also played a key role in Waterford's epochal 2002 win. The family ghost of 1982 has been well and truly laid to rest.

EPILOGUE

The renaissance of the Munster Championship continued in 2003 when the Cork public greeted victory with a fanaticism that hadn't been witnessed for several decades. Their team had taken a strange and twisting path to glory, beginning the season with a players' strike over what they felt was a lack of respect being shown them by the County Board. Once that had been settled, the Rebels were a reinvigorated force and their Munster campaign took on remarkable momentum.

After hammering Clare in the semi-final, they met a Waterford side determined to prove that the previous year's history-making success had been no fluke. Cork looked down-and-out when they trailed at half-time, but roared back to win by 3-16 to 3-12. Once more they had proven themselves adept at unearthing promising new players at the drop of a hat – Ronan Curran and Tom Kenny in the half-back line, John Gardiner at midfield and Setanta O'hAilpin, already these youngsters look like potential legends of the game.

The Cork bandwagon finally came to a halt when a great Kilkenny team beat them 1-14 to 1-11 in the All-Ireland final. That young, talented team looked set for greater things, but on the day it didn't go their way. That is the way of things in Munster. Every few years brings a new set of players to carry on the great tradition of Cork and Tipperary, while the hurling men of Clare, Waterford and Limerick plot ambushes against the über teams. That's how it should be. It would be a mistake to regard the story of Munster hurling as one of unrelieved Cork and Tipperary dominance. You can just never tell when the other three will make a breakthrough, and when they do, it's always in spectacular style. Limerick did it in the 1930s and 1970s, Waterford in the 1950s and 1960s and Clare, finally, in the 1990s. The Big Two are never able to rest on their laurels. For the fans, this is the lifeblood of the game: the unpredictability, the relish of the unexpected. There are many more mouth-watering days to come.

In the new millennium, the five great counties all have legitimate reason to hope that a bright future awaits them (Kerry, despite great efforts by a stalwart few, will have to be content with football honours for the foreseeable future): Tipperary were 2001 All-Ireland champions; Cork won the 2003 Munster Championship in great style; Waterford are newly buoyant and self-confident following their 2002 provincial win; Limerick have players from their phenomenal under-21 three-in-a-row team of 2000–2002 coming through; and Clare have remained in the top echelon since the Loughnane revolution. Munster has never been as democratic.

Looking over the whole history of Munster hurling, in many ways, ever since the first All-Ireland Championship in 1884, the country's hurlers have been playing one big match – fresher players taking over after their predecessors have given their all and headed for the bench. Everyone is connected.

The Munster Hurling Championship continues to be something unique, something valuable, something that brings out the best in people. The surviving heroes of the past have now handed the torch to the next generation, but those legendary men of the ash still take their place in the stands every summer, without fail, without exception. And although Christy Ring succumbed to a heart attack in 1979 and Mick Mackey passed away six years later, they're there too. They always will be.